"The incarnation, at the center of Christian faith, provides a touchstone for understanding the world as God's good creation and human beings as called to embodied, dialogical relationship with their creator. This ambitious book contrasts the incarnational Christian vision with contemporary permutations of ancient Gnosticism, teasing out philosophical implications of an incarnational spiritual culture for human identity in the twenty-first century."

—J. Richard Middleton
Professor of biblical worldview and exegesis,
Northeastern Seminary at Roberts Wesleyan University

"It's easy to see that we are in the grip of a cultural identity crisis! What's not so easy to see is a way out. Gordon Carkner provides both the head and heart knowledge necessary to ground our identity in Christ in such a way that leads to the flourishing of ourselves and our communities. I highly recommend this thoughtful and passionate engagement with today's most pressing challenge—our identity."

—Andy Steiger
Founder and president, Apologetics Canada

"This book develops a profound idea: that in the incarnation, God's glory and generosity have been revealed in Jesus as publicly accessible truth. Furthermore, the God who was incarnated invites us to try life with him. Be prepared for a provocative journey through several contemporary ideologies elucidated by the insights of philosopher Charles Taylor and other important thinkers. It may result in a deeper appreciation of the presence of the glorious creator whose signs of transcendence surround us."

—Paul Chamberlain
Professor of ethics and leadership, Trinity Western University

"Gordon Carkner surveys a wealth of philosophical literature and shares much of his own personal wisdom, showing clearly how strongly influenced our society is by modern versions of Gnosticism and how diametrically opposed that is to the biblical teaching of an incarnational life. An excellent book on a very timely topic which should be of interest to Christians and skeptics alike."

—Martin Ester
Distinguished professor of computing science, Simon Fraser University

"Having read widely and deeply in contemporary literature and philosophical thought, Gordon Carkner is able to alert us to the 'minefields' hidden along the highway of contemporary culture, especially contemporary Western culture. But this is not only a critique of that culture. Being deeply rooted in the Judeo-Christian faith, Carkner is also able to guide us to vistas of great grandeur embedded in the biblical account of creation and re-creation."

—Sven Soderlund
Professor emeritus of biblical studies, Regent College

"Gordon Carkner's latest book is an important work of theological anthropology examining the grounds for human dignity through the lens of the incarnation of Christ. Carkner dialogues with thinkers such as Charles Taylor who increase our articulate grasp of the issues and broaden our understanding of the incarnation as the epicenter for a *thick* identity, grounded in God and nurtured by grace. Such an identity prepares us for a robust engagement with, and critique of, late modern culture."

—Andrew Lawe
General surgeon and clinical instructor, UBC Southern Medical Program

"This reflective work by Gordon Carkner comes to us at a poignant moment. More than ever, people need to grapple with the grandeur, beauty, and coherence of the incarnation—the Jesus story. At its core, it is a transformative, reversal narrative, where prodigals and cynics are invited to become compassionate healing agents, committed to justice and mercy. This book offers a tremendous resource for pastors and church members who want to live the artfulness of agape love."

—Matthew Menzel
Lead pastor, Westside Church

Towards an Incarnational Spiritual Culture

Towards an Incarnational Spiritual Culture

Grounding Our Identity in Christ

by GORDON E. CARKNER

Foreword by IAIN PROVAN

WIPF & STOCK · Eugene, Oregon

Wipf & Stock
An Imprint of Wipf and Stock Publishers
199 W. 8th Ave., Suite 3
Eugene, OR 97401

www.wipfandstock.com

PAPERBACK ISBN: 979-8-3852-0377-2
HARDCOVER ISBN: 979-8-3852-0378-9
EBOOK ISBN: 979-8-3852-0379-6

VERSION NUMBER 012224

Dedicated to My Family

My dear wife Ute Carkner, my daughter Kierianne Slotman and her husband Lukas, and my daughter Hannah.

Contents

Foreword by Iain Provan | ix
Acknowledgments | xi
Introduction | xiii

1 Comparing Gnosticism to an Incarnational Stance | 1

2 God's Grand Invitation to Dialogue: Where Are You Speaking From? | 12

3 Jesus the Ground of Wisdom | 30

4 Incarnation: Individuals Engaged in Community | 54

5 Transcendent Goodness Meets the Good Society | 81

   Conclusion | 110

Addendum: What Do People Mean by a Personal Relationship with Jesus? | 115

Bibliography | 121

Foreword

WE LIVE IN A world marked by crises of various kinds, but perhaps most deeply and fundamentally by a crisis as to the nature of our humanity. What does it mean to be human?

For example, are human beings essentially *minds*, trapped temporarily and regrettably in physical bodies? Certainly many artificial intelligence enthusiasts see the world in precisely this way. Marvin Minsky, for example, believes that the mind is all that is really important about life, over against that *bloody mess of organic matter* that is the body. Out of this conviction arises another: that mind machines represent the next step in human evolution. We ourselves, in our godlike state, ought to create this new species—*Machina sapiens* instead of *Homo sapiens*—passing the torch of life and intelligence on to the computer (Rudy Rucker). Our ultimate goal is the conversion of "the entire universe into an extended thinking entity . . . an eternity of pure cerebration" (Hans Moravec).

From this single example we gather what should already be obvious to us in any case: that our governing ideas about human nature inevitably have significant consequences. They matter *individually*, affecting how I look at myself, what I agree to do to myself or have done to me, and the goals I set for myself. They also matter *communally*, affecting how I look at and treat other people, and what kind of society I am trying to help build. In fact, the answer to this question about humanness affects everything else that matters in life. And this means that arriving at good rather than bad answers to the question is a high-stakes game. It means that arriving at the *truth* of the matter is crucially important. Is it really true, for example, that we are essentially minds that *happen* to possess bodies that we may or may not consider satisfactory? If we can manage it, should the physical body be discarded like a piece of clothing in pursuit of something more glorious, with the help of technology?

It is into the very centre of this kind of contemporary discourse that Gordon Carkner has inserted this new book about *incarnational spiritual culture*, with a view to encouraging readers to ground *their identity in Christ*, rather than somewhere else. He invites us to consider the great difference between incarnational spiritual culture, on the one hand, and both ancient and modern anti-material *Gnosticisms*, on the other—rejecting the latter in favor of the former. He explores the incarnation of Christ as the center point of history, giving dignity to embodied persons everywhere, and enabling us to rethink human wisdom and knowledge. He pursues the implications of this incarnation for human community and communion, contrasting the contemporary *will-to-uniqueness* that tears us apart to the *will-to-community* that reintegrates us. And he discusses, finally, the transformative nature of divine goodness, and its necessity for healthy human freedom.

We need all the help we can get in remaining human in these markedly inhumane times. This volume draws on deep and varied resources in offering such help, and I know that many people will benefit from reading it.

Iain Provan
Founder of the Cuckoos Consultancy
Author of *Cuckoos in Our Nest: Truth and Lies about Being Human*

Acknowledgments

ONE NEVER OPERATES ALONE on such a project. Thus, there are numerous people that we want to appreciate for their input, draft reading, and advice. Professor and theologian John Webster, then of Christ Church, Oxford; and professor of philosophy Donn Welton of Stony Brook University in New York, as first and second readers respectively, offered wise direction of the research for my doctoral dissertation on the dialogue between Foucault and Taylor on the moral self. This discussion backgrounds the journey of the book. Much appreciation goes out to the scholars and graduate students at the Oxford Center for Mission Studies and the University of Wales who tested the fecundity of many of the concepts as they were being formulated. Over the years, the writer has had the privilege to know and engage with many faculty members at Universities of Guelph, Waterloo, Wilfrid Laurier and University of British Columbia, Simon Fraser University, Regent College, and Trinity Western University. They are too many to mention. However, certain faculty interlocutors stand out in one's memory as inspiring examples, sound and creative thinkers, scholars and scientists: Drs. David Matthews, Philip Hill, Olav Slaymaker, Judith Toronchuk, David Ley, Dennis Danielson, Martin Barlow, George Egerton, John Redekop, Craig Mitton, Tim Huh, John Owen, James Sire, Arnold Sikkema, Ron Dart, and Martin Ester. All have been exemplary in taking seriously both their faith and their scholarship. They have shown passion in their teaching and a deep respect for students—the nurture of minds and hearts. In terms of high-caliber dialogue on nonreligious campuses, great inspiration has been taken from the Pascal Lectures at University of Waterloo, the Faraday Institute of Science and Religion at Cambridge University, BioLogos in the USA, the Canadian Science and Christian Affiliation, Christians in Science in the UK, the American Scientific Affiliation, the Gifford Lectures in Edinburgh, and the Veritas Forum, which began at Harvard University. The

UBC Graduate and Faculty Christian Forum, over some thirty-five years, has empowered cross-disciplinary discussion on a wide variety of topics, integrating faith and academic learning at a very high level. We are grateful for the numerous internationally-renowned scholars and scientists who contributed to this series beginning with Sir John Polkinghorne of Queens' College, Cambridge. More names will be mentioned throughout the book. Credit must be attributed to the many bright students who have been a part of our lives and community over the decades of ministry. Their passion for scholarly excellence and energy for making a strong contribution to the common good is nothing short of inspirational. They helped to formulate and test ideas, and push the envelope in thinking Christianly. We highly value their curiosity and vision. Many thanks also go to the followers of the Graduate Christian Union blog (www.ubcgcu.org) who have field-tested many of my ideas and musings. The whole Outreach Canada team have been very supportive and constructive, including my supervisor, Executive Director Craig Kraft.

Introduction

THIS IS AN ACTIVE, lively investigation. Many people today are dissatisfied with the way things are. They want more than a mediocre, cynical life: more adventure and challenge, more truth and beauty, more joy and meaning. They want fresh vision to see better, think more clearly, and live at another level. The following discussion identifies with this quest and maps out a serious path, learning from centuries of wisdom on what it means to be a fully engaged human being. The goal of the book is to give us the ability to see, interpret, and experience reality with fresh eyes—discover a *re-enchantment* of reality. Recently, I watched the light of the early dawn over the Fraser River in Vancouver, Canada and my hope is that this discussion will bring that kind of fresh, brilliant light to your life as well as offering a critical realism that will ground you.

As we ascend to this higher way of life, we also want to escape the trap of restrictive ideologies that bog us down and stifle our imagination. They isolate us, divide us, encourage us not to think, even damage us. The *incarnational outlook* I propose in these pages has a scholarly reach that goes all the way back to Saint Augustine.[1] It is sourced in the Judeo-Christian biblical religion within a powerful, complex, and riveting narrative. The incarnation of Jesus the Messiah is irreducibly historical, as well as a turning point in world history. It is an event that splits time in two. Christopher Watkin notes that it involves the scandal of the particular, the material, and the personal.

> Whereas modernity privileges an unchanging ahistoricity, in the incarnation God enters history at a particular moment to gather a people to be with him not in a Greek eternity of unchanging

---

1. Smith, *On the Road with St. Augustine.*

timelessness but in a biblical eternity of never-ending and ever renewed intimacy and relational richness.[2]

This incarnational quest is an urgent priority for contemporary thought and life, promising breakthroughs and miraculous change. In the West, we are currently experiencing an existential crisis of identity which has us lonely, perplexed, and anxious. The integrative hermeneutic of incarnation will bring people together. It will push our limits and magnetically pull us forward as towards a true North—Christ. In my previous book, *The Great Escape from Nihilism*,[3] I mapped out a way to escape the philosophical and cultural traps and ideologies of early and late modernity. They reduce us to less, not more, than we intuitively know we are and can be, depriving us of meaning, value, and significance. In the following discussion, I want to elaborate a robust way forward beyond the walls of this same intellectual-spiritual-moral-identity prison. Cambridge theologian Andrew Davison notes wisely: "All that prepares for [incarnation], and follows from it, is a drama into which human life, history, and culture is gradually drawn."[4] In the process of this research and writing, I have been struck and so often overwhelmed by the gripping profundity of the task to capture the full implications of the incarnation. This quest has depth and breadth.

The journey begins as we set the stage in chapter 1 by comparing the gnostic outlook to Incarnational Spiritual Culture, including ancient and contemporary forms of Gnosticism. It is essential that we see the radical difference in worldviews that shape contemporary culture and vie for people's attention. This important comparison shows the big philosophical-theological picture. Several thinkers claim that late modern culture is like a rudderless ship adrift on a vast ocean or like a supernova of alternative spiritualities, filling people with confusion.

The discussion then proceeds in chapter 2 with a conversation, an *I-Thou* dialogue, a grand invitation by God to human beings. We are addressed by the transcendent within our time-space-energy-matter world—our *immanent frame*. This address or *call* does shock us out of our complacency and cynicism. Despite the current cacophony of conflicting voices, there is still a high degree of resonance with the Creator's invitation to dialogue, whether that occurs in our living room, or as with Moses before a burning bush. We are addressed, embraced, and invited to open

2. Watkin, *Biblical Critical Theory*, 367.

3. Carkner, *Great Escape from Nihilism*.

4. Davison, *Astrobiology and Christian Doctrine*, 311.

our hearts and minds to fresh wisdom and insight—with prospects of vital new experience. Much fruit is rendered as we with humble, teachable self-awareness move into new levels of attentiveness to our divine interlocutor. The prospects for this transcendent-immanent communication is written large in the incarnation. Jesus intimates in John chapter 14 that if people have seen him, they have brushed shoulders with ultimate reality. In fact, the incarnation of Jesus the Christ is one of the great gifts, God's grand masterpiece, the apogee of his *speech acts* (Col 1:15–17). It draws us into a new realization, a new legacy, and opens us to the reality of *epiphany*: divine love, grace, and merciful advocacy. The drama is artfully accommodated to human nature. We are talking about a situated, embodied first-century provincial Palestinian, Aramaic-speaking male carpenter, who also claimed to be the Alpha and Omega, God before all time, the one through whom all things were created. Incarnation is shown in the discussion before us to be relevant to human flourishing and dignity, personal resilience and spiritual wholeness.

Late moderns seem to want to either damage or deify their bodies. Christ marries the spiritual and the material in an intense act of identification with our human condition. God is beautifully present with us in a body like ours, with all its vulnerabilities and longings.

> He became a particular human, once more affirming the peculiar dignity of human persons. . . . To what higher end was humanity able to be raised than that a human being, consisting of a rational soul and human flesh, a human being, exposed to mortal accidents, dangers, and needs, in brief, a true and perfect man, inexplicably assumed in one person within the Word, the son of God, consubstantial with the Father and co-eternal with Him.[5]

Incarnation concerns both the Person and Work of Christ. No constitutive aspect of humanity was missing. He did not reveal himself as a disembodied spirit, an idea, principle, program, or set of laws. Therefore, from the highest source, he gave dignity to persons throughout the world. It is groundbreaking revelation.

In chapter 3, I open up the concept of Christ as the wisdom of God, a rethink of human wisdom and knowledge. Wisdom is something we all seek on a daily basis. The discourse in John chapter 1 speaks of Jesus as *Logos*, the divine Word taking on human flesh. For the apostle John, the *Logos* is more than reason, but a person: the *Logos* is no longer an idea in the

5. Watkin, *Biblical Critical Theory*, 364.

mind of the philosopher or the mystic. The *Logos* here is the man Jesus who went the way from Bethlehem to Calvary, who did many miracles and rose from the dead. These things and his present advocacy sealed the New Covenant. In the Christ, we have both immanence and transcendence, physical and spiritual, a grounded spirituality that brings heaven and earth together. Biblical scholar Anthony Thiselton[6] says that the mystery of the incarnation is too profound for human discovery by reason alone. Rather, he says that it requires *epiphany* or divine revelation. It is beyond our limited human imagination to conjure or invent. On the other hand, open-minded reasoning engages, and is engaged by, such profound epiphany—food for thought. We humans are more than capable of grappling with its implications. The right posture, the right intellectual virtues of humility and openness can result in discovering many new things about ourselves and our world. Incarnational spirituality is ultimately grounded in the wisdom of the ages, while offering a bright, redemptive future hope.

In chapter 4, I drill down into the implications of the incarnation for human community and communion. For this purpose, I compare and contrast philosophers Charles Taylor and Michel Foucault on constituting one's moral and spiritual identity either within or apart from community. The contrast illustrates two of the great forces at work in culture today: the will-to-uniqueness (*expressive individualism*) and the will-to-community (*one-anotherness*). These forces together with their concomitant decisions and choices either bring us together or tear us apart. I then show how the strong quest towards individual autonomy is handicapping people, making them vulnerable to cult heroes and strange ideas which seek to devour them. Incarnational spiritual culture opens us to the stability and resilience of healthy, honest, covenantal relationships. The incarnation is more mind-expanding and life-changing in its implications than many people realize. To mitigate the current identity crisis, I proceed to discuss the importance of our narrative selves as storied individuals in community, in search of a richer and stronger foundation for what we are capable to become.

Finally in chapter 5, the focus shifts to divine transcendent goodness as a transforming agency, a necessity for healthy human freedom. The gap between divine and human is great. We show how the incarnation brings a connection, or an interface between the transcendent and the immanent realms on the issues of goodness, ethics, and identity. *Agape* love gets major play at this juncture—revealing divine goodness in real time. It sparks a

6. Thiselton, *Interpreting God and the Postmodern Self.*

whole new set of power relations. This offers hope on how we are able to be transformed by divine goodness, bridging the finite-infinite gap. The Holy Spirit, sent by Jesus, is revealed to be God's great communicator and interpreter of his gracious gifts and infinite goodness to the world. The Holy Spirit is cosmic *gift* to the church. Thus, our discourse is trinitarian: the Father sends the Son, who sends the Spirit.

Thank you so much for taking this higher road with me. Perseverance, courage, and patience are in order if you wish to discover what you came for—the fulfillment of those deep personal and spiritual longings. I trust that you long for divine connection, for the highest and most enduring kind of identity. This investigation could indeed move your universe and transform the people nearest and dearest to you. When one puts in the effort to travel the higher road, a new appreciation for, and a new perspective on reality emerges. I believe that your curiosity will be greatly rewarded. Like in the *Camino de Santiago* reflective pilgrimage, we must reckon with our fears and hesitations, and then set them in perspective as we begin to courageously and creatively claim a powerful discovery of life lived large. There is here an enduring legacy in Christ the Lord of the Universe, the very Author of Life—he was one of us. It most likely will involve suffering and struggle to get to the full, radical truth of the matter and land on solid ground, as Parker Palmer reflects in *Let Your Life Speak*.[7]

7. Palmer, *Let Your Life Speak*.

1

Comparing Gnosticism
to an Incarnational Stance

PART I. CHARTING A CONTRAST IN OUTLOOK.

THERE ARE MANY DIFFERENT types of Gnosticism today. Thus, it is helpful
to compare various certainties about knowledge as well as radical uncertainty or skepticism (agnosticism). Below we chart a comparison between
the ancient and modern forms of Gnosticism with incarnational spiritual
culture. Culture is more than theory, it involves symbols, values, and practices, habits of the heart, the mind, and ultimately one's lifestyle. This results
in a whole outlook that Charles Taylor calls a *social imaginary*.[1]

---

1. I would like to thank Mark Sayers, *Disappearing Church*, 64. for the basic idea of
this comparison between ancient and modern Gnosticism and Christianity. This chart is
my articulation, using my philosophical-theological concepts.

Ancient Gnosticism	Contemporary Gnosticism	Incarnational Spirituality
Worldview: The physical world is lesser or lower in status.	Your world and your body are inadequate, blocking your fulfilment. It must be fixed, improved, or escaped.	Creation is good and beautiful in itself, although broken relationships have resulted from the rebellion of humans. Christ has restored these, but creation still groans towards its full redemption (Rom 8). It is a world in process of healing, with a mixture of good and evil.
The Problem: Matter is the issue. We must fear and fight against our lower *bestial* nature.	The average is the stumbling block. Boredom is bad and must be resisted at all cost.	Sin, brokenness, disobedience, and rebellion are the issue, creating a bad relationship with a loving Creator, conflict with oneself and with creation: a full-fledged alienation.
The Solution: You must escape your body to enhance your spirit, to reach the heights of self. Ascend towards the Light.	Tune your body into a wonder, get a makeover or surgery. Take your life to the edge of thrills and adventure. Release yourself from inhibitions and fully express your desires.	Jesus's gift of grace offers freedom from sin, guilt, and shame. He is the incarnate Son of Man, a fully free life of servanthood. There should be no fear or disgust towards one's body—it is God's temple. Humans are soulish/spiritual bodies, embodied beings, embedded in social networks and relationships. There is healing available for the whole person and for culture. God loves every aspect of us.
Start Here: Search to find the truth and the god within, to find that fragment of a divine spark remnant in you at creation.	Discover the real you and reach towards your full potential. You can be all that you desire to become with the right therapy, advice, and specific modifications.	God opens our eyes to fullness of being human, wisdom, virtue, and reality, the true nature of things. Salvation is *this-worldly*, including *all things*: matter, bodies, relationships, morality, institutions, education, society, politics, and culture.

COMPARING GNOSTICISM TO AN INCARNATIONAL STANCE

Ancient Gnosticism	Contemporary Gnosticism	Incarnational Spirituality
Human Flourishing: Rise above this inadequate world for a higher, perfect spiritual space or plane of existence.	Leave behind the bland existence for the most amazing experience of your life. You can have it all right now. Avoid commitments that restrict your freedom, choices, discoveries, or your self-actualization.	There is wonder, hope, deep meaning, creativity, and purpose in worship and service to God and his kingdom agenda within this time-space *immanent* frame. Spirituality is embodied, worship of God (not the world) is corporate. The incarnation shows an interface of the transcendent and immanent in the God-man Jesus, and within the body of Christ, the church. Healing is offered for our many failures.
The Process: You can move beyond all flaws and inadequacies through finding special hidden knowledge (*gnosis*) from a guru, shaman, or special spirit guide.	Strive towards the ideal body, marriage, and career through online gurus, self-help secrets of success. Self-create or re-invent yourself (Foucault) as you choose to be. Change your gender as you feel best suits you. Be unique (an original) and by all means love yourself first.	Seek God as your first priority. Pursue righteousness, justice, wholeness, truth, Christlike virtues. Pursue full social and communal redemption within this world. Cultivate kindness, forgiveness, and reconciliation here and now. Look forward to the eventual full interface of heaven on earth with its resurrected, glorified bodies when the world's redemption will reach its final *apogee*—the eschaton.

Ancient Gnosticism	Contemporary Gnosticism	Incarnational Spirituality
Human Identity: You are on a journey, pursuing higher spiritual truths and hidden knowledge through special mystical or magical technologies. You must always try to avoid imploding into the bestial, lower self.	You are in quest of a better life through exciting experiments, experiences and pleasures: travel, romance, fun, adventure, extreme sports, social media, video games, artificial intelligence, genetic or surgical manipulation. Upload your brain to a digital database for eternal life. Dionysius is your inspiration as you express yourself as a unique individual.	You are the grateful recipient of profound common grace (creation) and special grace (Jesus's redemptive work on the cross). You are deeply loved by God (covenant love); he knows your name. You were never destined to be a god, but you can become a whole human being. Christ will help mediate your relationship with God to make it fruitful and abundant. The Holy Spirit will guide you into all truth in this embodied, socially embedded life. Make God the first love in your life so that you can mediate his presence and joy within this culture. Practice Jesus's Lordship and humble obedience to find true freedom.
The Way of Salvation: You must surpass the inferior god (demiurge) to find the real god—which is you after all. Lose your individual self in the infinite One, the All or Absolute.	Move beyond organized religion, moral norms, and traditional codes of behavior and thought. Find the type of spirituality that suits you. Doctrine, Bibles, or religious sources are not important. *Be spiritual but not religious.* Accessorize your life with a variety of things and activities to see what works best for you.	The Creator God wants to partner with you in his mission through the church: the concrete presence of the incarnation of God's Messiah on earth. Model the character of humility, fruits, and gifts of the Spirit within a healthy body of believers, a healing and witnessing community that is rooted in *agape* love . Become a godly citizen and a loving, hospitable neighbor. Live into your new story as part of God's great drama of salvation anticipating Jesus's second coming. Give glory and honor to God in everything you do.

COMPARING GNOSTICISM TO AN INCARNATIONAL STANCE

Ancient Gnosticism	Contemporary Gnosticism	Incarnational Spirituality
Practical Steps: Break past all the boundaries and limitations left in you by the inferior creator (*demiurge*), and become fully divine yourself.	Move past the restrictions of tradition, religion, and authorities. Through innovation, seek your own unique, *authentic* spiritual path.	Gain wisdom and self-giving skill through a community of believers writing a new story of kingdom values: integrity, joy, promise, caring, peace, and hope. Find your calling and use your gifts to promote *shalom*. Practice faithful presence, love your enemies, and live humbly with your neighbor. Become truly free, be a peacemaker and take responsibility for others. Learn to flourish within God's economy of grace.
The Transformation: When you finally arrive at this higher spiritual plane, you will discover that you are the god you have been searching for all along. Nothing can stop you now. You transcend the world and all limitations.	Life's meaning is all about your passion, your subjective feelings and sensibilities, your entitlements. Be all that you can be, that unique self that the internet and social media loves, even if it is quirky.	A New Vision: God's story of loving redemption for individuals, families, the culture and the planet is key to your identity. One is properly human with limits, but with a high calling to steward the earth as restored *imago Dei*. You are part of a counterculture. Jesus is the God-man at the right hand of the Father, interceding for you and your network of relations. Jesus sent the Holy Spirit to gift, empower, and encourage you. He will return to bring fulfillment to all human beings seeking spiritual wholeness. His death on the cross and resurrection remain the climax of God's redemptive narrative, a model of humble servanthood and suffering love for a broken world.

PART II. GNOSTIC SPIRITUALITY: DIS-INCARNATE RELIGION DEFINED

Four Working Assumptions and Seven Theological Markers

1. Modern Gnosticism is a highly individualistic quest for personal and spiritual self-invention or reinvention. One senses the need to seek one's own individual destiny—to become a god or goddess. This contains the goal of a higher spiritual plane than traditional religion— moving towards the Light—a higher plane than scientific knowledge. What is at stake is the primacy of self, choice, personal freedom, and self-actualization. One is shooting for the higher, enlightened self and thus one must consume various spiritual experiences and learn spiritual technologies along the way. Gurus offer special knowledge for the journey, known as spiritual secrets (*Gnosis*). How I feel about myself and how I define myself is critically important to this endeavor. I must transcend groups, institutions, and covenants that try to define me. At core, Gnosticism is the gospel of *self-idolization*. It is a race to the top through performance: towards aspirations such as incredible wealth, success, happiness, or bliss. Salvation, according to Christianity, is all about transformation of the inner person who is embedded in many social and familial relations.

2. The world we live in appears inferior to the gnostic: flawed, broken, dark, chaotic, and confusing. In essence, *god the creator (the demiurge), did a bad job*. It is the world that holds us back from our true and ultimate spiritual fulfilment. Some gnostics believe that both the physical world and matter are actually evil. They are confining and restrictive with respect to the soul—issuing into a dualistic anthropology. A war breaks out between body and soul which plays out in various aspects of Western culture. The individual must transcend all this pain, suffering, struggle, and tragedy by means of disengagement from the world. They must retreat or withdraw, losing their desire for the world. The spiritual is above (outside of) the physical world; matter is of little consequence. This aforementioned world is not our true home but an alien, offensive place into which we have been tragically thrown (Heidegger). Hell is other people (Sartre) meaning that society is the problem, not me.

3. To flourish, one must escape the world, with its confines and restrictions, for a new utopia, a new ideal form of existence. To reach this goal, one must transgress given limits: gender, sex, white male domination, colonialism, divine moral tenets, family, institutions, and societal norms. The escape can involve travel to other planets, drugs, extreme sports, extreme makeovers, or special lifestyles. The job is to become an *original*, a revolutionary. This has led some into loss of discernment regarding good and evil, right and wrong—with the attendant victimization of the innocent and vulnerable. Utopias always have their marginalized victims. Others have become susceptible to cult leaders, dictators, health and wealth gospelers, and Ponzi schemes. The irony is that radical individualism can make one more vulnerable to ideology, grifters, and manipulators. Some egregious crimes have been perpetrated by gnostic leaders and gurus. Cult leaders often take people away from their normal social network and accountability structure. At core, there seems to be a fundamental denial of death[2] at work, with a built-in unwillingness to struggle in life or to suffer.

4. The Gnostic Ghost: We discover in this admixture a sacrifice of true personhood for a fantasy world of one's own creation. Dreams are synonymous with reality; conspiracy theories are taken as credible information. There is a deep dissatisfaction and impatience with the paradoxes, complexities, and vexations of human existence. The *Gnostic Ghost* often projects an abstracted image of self through a monologue of strong rhetoric. Entailed in this posture is a *commitment-phobia*. That entails a rebellion against moral code, personal responsibility, and sacrifice for the other (the common good). The gnostic is involved in a revolution of release from restraint. Freedom of choice is of the essence and consumerism is at the forefront of mind. One finds in the ghost an obsession with continual change and a passion to accessorize. Examples can be found within the New Age Movement to include hair color, tattoos, clothing, jewelry, and crystals, plus various meditation techniques. But all this can leave the individual feeling isolated, lonely, disengaged, and fragile. To be human is to suffer and to carry uncertainty about many things outside one's control. Relationships are often complex and take much diligent work and thought.

---

2. Becker, *Denial of Death*. He is an American cultural anthropologist.

Theological Articulations of Gnosticism in Hans Urs von Balthasar: Seven Markers

The concepts below are articulated with the help of two Balthasar scholars, Kevin Mongrain[3] and Raymond Gawronski (*Word and Silence*).[4] Gnosticism chooses mysticism over mystery, aesthetic mythologies (ideology of the aesthetic) over incarnational revelation, negation of personality over uniqueness of persons, resigned agnosticism over affirmation of the Word (who claimed to be the Truth), the nothingness of Nirvana over fullness of being. One other contrast is between the ascent of the human versus the descent of God. This is a brief but significant overview of the theological issues:

1. Gnosticism prefers ahistorical, "*a priori* myths or speculative theories over against the historically contingent events or the biblical narratives."[5] For examples of such epic positions, see Hegel's philosophy of Absolute Spirit. Karl Marx invented his secular utopia of communism with the ruling proletariat and the mythology of a *new man* based on Hegelian dialectical materialism. The dark side is the blood of revolution and government theft of property.

2. Gnosticism "rejects the belief that the divine transcends the categories of human thinking, and hence believes that the divine can be conceptually mastered in *a priori* theories"[6] (Neo-Platonism, nineteenth-century German idealism, materialistic naturalism, pantheism, or panentheism). It is highly abstract and rationalistic.

3. Gnosticism "is inherently disdainful of the Christian claim that the eternal God entered time, became incarnate in a human being, suffered, died and was resurrected as a spiritual body."[7] Believing in a larger gap between the human and divine realms, it relies on mysticism to cross the gap. The gnostic worldview tends to see YHWH, the Creator, as beneath it, to see Jesus as a created *aeon* or a much lower divine being. Hubris arises from the theory that there is a *God* behind God (a Monad), an unknown abyss behind the Creator God, a hidden

---

3. Mongrain, *Systematic Thought of Balthasar*, 33–37
4. Gawronski, *Word and Silence*.
5. Mongrain, *Systematic Thought of Balthasar*, 34.
6. Mongrain, *Systematic Thought of Balthasar*, 34.
7. Mongrain, *Systematic Thought of Balthasar*, 36.

Light at the top. Ultimate Being (The One) is taken as hidden and ineffable.

4. Gnosticism "gives rise to a variety of alternative religious systems, all of which attempt to look behind Christ presented in canonical Scriptures and the church in order to explain the meaning of redemption in terms of *a priori* metaphysical laws."[8] Humans must save themselves through knowledge. Two types of self-redemption exist: a. Dualist—the soul must escape the material world (often seen as evil); b. Monist—it offers enlightenment through a grand universal theory (rationalism, scientism, pantheism, aestheticism, evolutionism). It dispels all differences, all relatives in favor of the supremacy of the Absolute. UK Chief Rabbi Johnathan Sacks speaks to this problem in his *The Dignity of Difference*.[9]

5. The gnostic view is that "the meaning of Christ is not glorification of creation but instead negation of creation in its materiality, temporality and multiplicity."[10] The individual must *excarnate* herself and escape into a more ultimate, ahistorical, otherworldly realm.

6. Gnosticism is often "elitist and extremely ascetic because . . . salvation depends on attaining knowledge and mastery of specific techniques for the soul to escape the body and/or the realm of illusion."[11] This makes it secretive and insular, open only to the specially initiated, power-oriented people like Yale University's *Skull & Bones Society* or the Masons. Michel Foucault's ethics on the care of self as a work of art, which we cover in chapter 4, also displays this elitist, self-mastery element (*technology of self*). Zen was the tradition of the elite in China and Japan, and now in the post-Christian West.

7. Discursive thought or *I-Thou* dialogue is spurned.[12] God the Creator is scorned in favor of *silence*—which is present with God *above* or *behind* God. It involves a monological movement of self-explanation, self-invention, and self-divinization. The individual becomes one with ultimate being or non-being as in Zen.

---

8. Mongrain, *Systematic Thought of Balthasar*, 36.
9. Sacks, *Dignity of Difference*.
10. Mongrain, *Systematic Thought of Balthasar*, 37.
11. Mongrain, *Systematic Thought of Balthasar*, 37.
12. Gawronski, *Word and Silence*, 142.

The central assertion of Gnosticism is that there is an essential connection between the human and divine spirits. God and the human spirits are so ontically fused that self-knowledge is equivalent to knowledge of God. Therefore, faith is superfluous and the key element is *gnosis* or knowledge. There is little or nothing in Gnosticism regarding the centrality of justice and peacemaking, public responsibility, civic virtues and politics, ecological concerns and the importance of place, time and history. One sees a refusal to take responsibility for the world and the common good. Gnosticism also involves the trajectory of the *via negativa*[13] negative theology ultimately landing us in the silence of nihilism, the *un-word*. Zen is the apex in Asia of such negative theology: absolute nothingness, Non-Being or Nirvana = Samsara.

Zen represents the most extreme attempt to escape the limits of the human condition. It implies annihilation of God, humankind, and the world. Raymond Gawronski summarizes the problem that Balthasar astutely recognizes, which is a radical religious nihilism where the Absolute is ineffable and silent.

> Natural man tries to escape from this world of limitation, finitude, death. Individualistic schemes of salvation lead him to dissolve his individual humanity or to dissolve his ties with the rest of humanity in attempts at union with the Absolute. In the end, all systems of natural religion or religious philosophy are based on attempts at identity. Without the revelation that comes from a personal God, a personal Absolute, reason tends to take over and reason projects itself as a monologue, the union is ultimately with oneself. . . . One is in danger of losing both the world and God. There remains absolute emptiness, the *Undgrund*, Nirvana. . . . The ascent is always the way of silence [negation].[14]

The spiritual vacuum left by a technological society seems to have created the hunger for such religious systems as Zen in the West. The Western soul is searching for anything spiritual after becoming technologized and *soulless* to the point of emptiness. Having rejected Christianity during the Enlightenment, the gnostic individual seeks a controllable *spirituality without religion*—typical of Millennials and Generation Z. Balthasar is sharp to connect the gnostic outlook of nineteenth-century German idealism and

---

13. Gawronski, *Word and Silence*, esp. ch. 2, pp. 75–132. This is one of his brilliant insights into Gnosticism.

14. Gawronski, *Word and Silence*, 69–70.

eastern religions like Zen. There is also a link between Neo-Platonism and Buddhism: Balthasar confirmed my suspicion about this. This is part of the quest to be one in identity with ultimate being and lose one's individual self in the process. Britain's Jewish public intellectual, Jonathan Sacks, spoke of Plato's problematic influence on contemporary Western culture in his very insightful volume *The Dignity of Difference*, especially the chapter entitled "Dignity of Difference: Exorcizing Plato's Ghost."[15] He contrasts Platonism to the biblical God. He believes that Platonism contributes to many cultural problems such as tribalism and clash of civilizations.

> He [God] is a particularist, loving each of his children for what they are. . . . God, author of diversity, is the unifying presence within diversity. . . . A God of your side as well as mine must be a God of justice who stands above us both, teaching us to make space for one another, to hear each other's claims and resolve them equitably. Only such a God would be truly transcendent—greater not only than the natural universe but also than the spiritual universe, capable of being comprehended in any human language, from any single point of view. Only such a God can teach mankind to make peace other than by conquest and conversion, and as something nobler than practical necessity.[16]

In the end, Gnosticism is a failed attempt to answer the big existential human questions of longing for God, personal transformation, guilt of existence, identity, shame, suffering, and death. Its spirituality is *excarnate* and otherworldly, truly escapist in orientation. It wants to leave this disenchanted world of mere materiality. This brief overview gives us a frame for our discussion. It will lead to some thoughtful debate and dialogue about the contrast between incarnational and gnostic spiritual culture. We will return to many of these issues throughout the book, admitting that there are aspects not covered. For example, German-American political philosopher Eric Voegelin has much more to say about political Gnosticism and ideology.[17]

---

15. Sacks, *Dignity of Difference*, 45–66.
16. Sacks, *Dignity of Difference*, 56, 65.
17. Voegelin, *Science, Politics and Gnosticism*; Voegelin, *New Science of Politics*.

2

God's Grand Invitation to Dialogue
Where Are You Speaking From?

PART I. THE CALL TO DIALOGUE

SPEAKING IS INDEED A creative act. It includes both a discovery of self and a self-constitution. It is within this economy of discourse that the self is called into being as the *who* that is speaking and listening, writing, and reading. Humans are speaking agents in a variety of situations and modalities of discourse. To be a self is to be able to render an account of oneself, to be able to tell the story of one's life. "The self is implicated in its discourse as a 'who' that is at the crossroads of speech and language," writes philosopher Calvin Schrag.[1] This language is part of a tradition and history that we find ourselves in as we grow and develop. This is why autism is so devastating for an individual. The biblical narrative is all about a transcendent God who engages humans in lively conversation. God confronts us, engages us, calls us out, as he did with Abraham and Moses. He initiates a breach in the cosmic silence. But are we listening?

Why are we here? Where have we come from? What is our calling or purpose? Where are we going? Who are we really working for? What do we love? These are some of the key existential, life-challenging questions. How do we make sense of justice, freedom, power, and relationships? Why do we suffer and experience violence in our world? Where do we find meaning,

---

1. Schrag, *Self after Postmodernity*, 17

hope, and joy? Religion at its heart attempts to answer such questions of meaning, identity, longing (*Sehnsucht*), guilt, suffering, and death. Such questions take us deeper into our human consciousness as the *religious animal*. French philosophical theologian Paul Ricoeur, famous for his work on the narrative self, often asked his graduate students in their research to answer the question, "Where are you speaking from?" What is your story and the backstory of your research? This perhaps remains one of the most vital questions. Our best friends often ask us the most probing questions. Spiritual theologian Eugene Peterson speaks to the heart of this concern:

> God's word to us is essentially a call, an invitation, a welcome into his presence and action. When we respond to the call, we live a calling. The calling gives us a destination, determines what we do, shapes our behavior, forms a coherent life. We live into the world and the relationships into which we have been called. . . . Vocation, calling, is a way of life, comprehensive. . . . God's call and our calling fuse into church. The call and calling are the systolic and diastolic heartbeat of the body of Christ.[2]

In order to compose this book, I had to upgrade my thinking and my questions. Despite certain common beliefs of secularity, the eminent Canadian philosopher Charles Taylor explains that science has not replaced religion in late modernity in his famous tome *A Secular Age*.[3] In fact, we humans remain quite *haunted* by transcendence. Brilliant Jewish writer Abraham Joshua Heschel contends that God has not given up on humankind. He continues to show an interest in our wellbeing, to take initiative, to provoke us out of our complacency, our existential sleepiness.

> Man is more than what he is to himself. In his reason he may be limited, in his will he may be wicked, yet he stands in a relation to God which he may betray but not sever, and which constitutes the essential meaning of life. He is the knot in which heaven and earth are interlaced. God in the universe is a spirit of concern for life. . . . We often fail in trying to understand him not because we do not know how to extend our concepts far enough, but because we do not know how to begin close enough. To think of God is not to find him as an object in our minds, but to find ourselves in him.[4]

2. Peterson, *Practice Resurrection*, 169–70.

3. Taylor, *Secular Age*. Taylor refuses to see the time-space world as the extent of reality.

4. Heschel, *Wisdom of Heschel*, 20, 329.

The individual human is addressed by God personally, as in Martin Buber's famous I-Thou articulation. Here's how Raymond Gawronski puts it: "It is God's calling the individual by name that gives each one his unique worth. . . . It is the unlimited 'I' of God that calls the limited 'I' of man into existence."[5] My "I" is a "Thou" for God; I can only become an "I" because God acts as my "Thou." Human and divine realities are dialogically linked in a very significant way. "One can only become an 'I' as awakened by the love of the 'Thou.'"[6] This can be seen in the call of Abraham, the burning bush of Moses, the entreaties of Hebrew prophets for moral, cultural, and spiritual reform. Or we might think of the call of teenage Mary to participate in a very special birth as an instrument of incarnation. There is an attraction upward into a stretching dialogue with our divine interlocutor while keeping our feet planted on *terra firma*. We are strongly encouraged to reason and commune with our Creator: "Where are you, Adam?" Lone individuals are identified, loved, valued, nurtured, embraced, and included in the leadership of God's great redemptive narrative. The divine fox continues his endless pursuit of us.

> "The Christ" stood for the presence of God in the world. . . . Paul felt he had discovered something crucial—the supreme moral fact about humans—which provided the basis for reconstructing human identity, opening the way to what he called "a new creation." . . . In Paul's eyes, the Christ reveals God acting through human agency and redeeming it. . . . Through an act of faith in the Christ, human agency can become the medium of God's love— which Paul sometimes calls "faith acting through love."[7]

These *perlocutionary events*[8] are speech acts that produce an unavoidable impact on those addressed. God is the one who knows us best, knows our full potential, while calling us into a higher purpose. I agree with Swiss theologian Hans Urs von Balthasar, who sees the Word of God revealed in three rich and powerful ways, three speech acts: in creation, in the biblical narrative or Scripture, and most poignantly in the incarnation of Jesus of Nazareth. Each offers a powerful language usage that complements the others. It would take a lot of intentional effort, diversion, and deception to miss

5. Gawronski, *Word and Silence*, 142.

6. Gawronski, *Word and Silence*, 142.

7. Siedentop, *Inventing the Individual*, 58–59.

8. Refers to the force of getting someone to act or change: to persuade, convince, enlighten, inspire.

these vital discourses. Each speech act is an invitation to an *I-Thou* encounter which issues forth in a discovery, an *epiphany*. Working in conjunction, they constitute a most powerful resource for human culture, imagination, and inspiration. Each is laden with meaning, value, and weightiness. Each speech act engages with the big questions. By their light, we can make good sense of the world—*theos, cosmos, anthropos* (the divine, the physical world, and humanity). Our engagement with these speech acts involves engaging big blue sky thinking. Although it is often challenging, our participation in the conversation that follows means that we are willing to *face reality at all cost*. American Psychiatrist Scott Peck has argued that this constitutes the trajectory of mental and emotional health.[9]

In the context of the biblical narrative, the incarnation contains a wide explanatory range for late modern people. It reads backwards into historical memory,[10] it reads presently in our personal experience,[11] and it reads forwards[12] into our future, our destiny or *eschaton*. This journey into incarnational culture offers an *epiphany* or revelatory encounter for those keen to attend to transcendent speech. For us to become fully human, we must be open to being addressed by God. As the pinnacle of God's engagement with humanity, the incarnation's call to dialogue is nothing short of groundbreaking. It crowns the extraordinary dignity of life on earth. God poured himself into the body of a first-century Palestinian carpenter. Alister McFadyen illuminates some important nuances of its character. In Jesus of Nazareth, one sees God communicating and relating, not as a tyrannical, coercive, absolute sovereign. The incarnation shows Jesus as a vulnerable human, a humble suffering servant, as someone who was one of us, who experiences and empathizes with our pain (Phil 2). He fully identifies with our human condition:

> [By] incarnation in the body of the crucified one implies that God's freedom does not, after all, entail a transcendent aloofness from the world, but a form of involvement with it in which the divine being and freedom are staked. God subjects Godself to the risks, vulnerabilities and ambiguities of historical existence, including the risk of rejection, suffering and death, as well as of misinterpretation. God's freedom and sovereignty must be of a radical kind:

9. Peck, *Road Less Travelled.*
10. Peterson, *Jesus Way.*
11. Yancey, *Jesus I Never Knew.*
12. Wright, *Surprised by Hope.*

> the freedom to give oneself in relation; to be with and in creation
> in ways that are costly to God, but which do not abrogate God's
> sovereignty, freedom and transcendence.[13]

This brings engagement between divine freedom of self-giving *agape* love with the freedom of human beings embedded within history, right in the midst of their various culture spheres: science, ethics, aesthetics, and religion. The communication is multifaceted, multidimensional, and deeply impactful. Divine love is completely free love rooted in God's infinite goodness. In the Messianic narrative, one is confronted with a divine power that is thoroughly personal and grace-filled, exhibiting redemptive strength amidst vulnerability, and the tragedy of the cross. The incarnation deeply affirms human personhood: God is tri-personal, the very wellspring of personhood. Jesus is God-in-person at our door. He did not reveal himself as a disembodied spirit, a mere idea or ideal, nor a mysterious object or spiritual technology.

Incarnation displays divine hospitality that consequently has impact through forms of interpersonal communication and personal *presence*. It is less a divine monologue of commands, and more a hospitable dialogue in which humans are attended to, and respected, as subjective players and interlocutors in their own right. This includes the valued freedom of choice, possibility of refusal, and personal creativity. Within this freedom, humans are encouraged to ask questions, discern, and wrestle with divine speech in creation, Scripture, and in the profound *theodrama* of the incarnation. In the end, each person has to decide what to do with the Christ and his radical claims. It should be emphasized here that human agents are first *sought by*, and only then can they become *seekers of*, God. The Creator invites us to coffee.

The claim is that through the course of this dialogue, the closer one comes to the Son by heeding his call, in line with faith, the more unique one becomes—moving towards wholeness. One becomes more fully human and spiritually alive. Jesus, the *God-man*, pulls all God's self-expression together and reveals it to us. From the dawn of creation to the Beatitudes to the silence of the tomb, it is central to the incarnation that God can and does fully reveal himself (John 1:1–18). He is the Word above all words, the *superword*. "The Gospel Word is not just uttered words, but rather the whole fleshly existence of Jesus is the *interpretation* of the Father."[14] For the

13. McFadyen, *Sins of Praise*, 42.

14. Gawronski, *Word and Silence*, 168.

apostle John, the *Logos* is more than Greek reason or moral order; it is the man Jesus who traveled from Bethlehem to Calvary, grace enfleshed in a profound life.

> All the fragments of reality, all the words, are drawn to him as metal shavings are to a magnet. He is the primordial Word before all words—the *Urwort*—who as sharing in the divine essence is also an *Überwort*, the *alpha* and *omega*. . . . In the flesh, he speaks words, fragments themselves which are cast out like a net to gather the original fragments, turned away from their *telos* by misused human freedom, leading them not to destruction, but to fullness.[15]

Gawronski is so articulate here: Jesus is the sufficient and complete expression of God in this dialogue.

We must grapple with this knowledge to the deepest depths. No matter how tempting it may be to bypass the ambiguities of the finite, material, bodily, and temporal in favor of the purely spiritual and eternal understanding of redemption, we must refrain. Materiality and embeddedness are vital. Humans have no better access to spiritual meaning and truth than those embodied by the incarnate Christ's redemptive role in human history. He is the *apogee* of divine revelation, built on top of creation while integrated with creation, embedded within the narrative of Abraham and his descendants. Salvation, according to the incarnational way, is intentionally this-worldly and anthropological (Rom 8). It validates material reality, while warning us away from worshipping things. Indeed, it provides an antidote to idolatry.

> The analogy of this dramatic role provides a resource for indicating that the gift of redemption in the Christ-event does not supersede humanity's embodied nature or creation's horizontal history. Rather it irradiates them with spiritual meaning by glorifying the full nature of created human persons, enabling them to glorify God in return by sharing in Christ's temporal mission of redemption.[16]

In redeeming the created order, Christ redeems all social relationships that are intrinsic to human nature—all of culture, all races. In Jesus, we have revealed to us the holiness of one transparent life of love, both divine and human. Love, humility, sacrifice, and servant leadership are central to the Jesus story as we will see moving forward in the discourse of incarnational

15. Gawronski, *Word and Silence*, 188.
16. Mongrain, *Systematic Thought of Balthasar*, 196.

spirituality. It offers solidarity with the human condition as well as an exemplar for elevating our human existence to a new level. It truly dignifies humanity as a good.

> The [Christian] faith accepting that love amounted to an inner crucifixion, from which could emerge a transformed will, embodied in the person of Jesus. For Paul it was a personal transaction, the creation of another, better self. . . . It is an invitation to see a deeper self, an inner union with God. It offers to give reason itself a new depth. Rationality loses its aristocratic connotations. It is associated not with status and pride but with a humility which liberates.[17]

Philosophical theologian Christopher Watkin puts it even more powerfully in his *Biblical Critical Theory*.

> Love is the epicenter of the distinctively Christian way of being in the world—not power, respect, or tolerance, not equality, justice, freedom, enlightenment, or submission. Love is the overall shape of Christian ethics, the form of human participation in the created order. . . . Love sets the rules for how that world is structured and functions in its entirety. . . . Love is a way of being in and experiencing the world, approaching friends and enemies alike as people to be loved. . . . It is the warp and woof of Christian relationships. . . . Love is the signature disposition of Christ's disciples.[18]

The problems inherent in the narrow social imaginary of naturalistic secularity urges us to listen to the I-Thou dialogue of the incarnation. Western culture has hit a wall in many ways, as Regent College religion and culture scholar Jens Zimmermann notes in his *Incarnational Humanism*.[19] He argues that a proper Christian focus on the incarnation heads off a host of early and late modern philosophical issues, while stimulating a vision of a recovered humanism, a robust philosophical anthropology, and an enlightened spirituality. We hear more on this later in chapter 3.

British intellectual John Milbank is often found arguing that science was never meant to become a worldview, such as in *exclusive humanism*.[20] He is correct. Science is properly a self-limited methodology, a tool for discovering certain things about the physical dimensions of the world, in

17. Siedentop, *Inventing the Individual*, 58–60.

18. Watkin, *Biblical Critical Theory*, 390.

19. Zimmermann, *Incarnational Humanism*.

20. A term coined by Charles Taylor. See Milbank, *Theology and Social Theory*.

particular secondary causes. Science seeks to understand how and why things happen as they do, according to the natural processes of created reality. While very significant in its own right, science and empirical reason requires a larger context, a metaphysics, and other layers of meaning in order to flourish.

Incarnational theology states that God acts in all the natural processes (providence), amidst the existence and action of every creature. Good science operates on several vital assumptions that it cannot prove through scientific methodology. This is often missed by scientific commentators who venture into metaphysics.[21] We discuss this important point in a YouTube lecture in our GFCF lecture series: "Science and Scientism" with Oxford Physicist Ard Louis.[22] Unfortunately, contemporary science has been *hacked* by the ideology of *scientism* in the minds of many educated people. This deception leads some to even question reason itself, to nihilism and the consequential loss of choice and dignity. Nihilism starts with the loss of higher meaning, then it turns into unhappiness and ultimately into a deprivation of being—a reduction of one's full potential.[23] Ultimately, nihilism often leads to violence against oneself or others. But divine purposes, included in the incarnation, are achieved in a way that respects and upholds the integrity of creaturely entities and processes. Individuals restricted in their thinking by scientism find it difficult to tune in to the *grand conversation* of the incarnation—also crucial to Western culture's commitment to human rights. Some folks are *blinded by scientism* and trapped intellectually and imaginatively within the immanent frame.[24]

Even while consciously living within the immanent frame of late modernity, our hearts often long for transcendence, meaning, and purpose, that is if we have not already settled for a Closed World System.[25] We long for more, want to reach outside of this box of thought, realizing that scientific understanding is not enough for full humanity and fulsome spirituality. Oxford literary scholar C. S. Lewis is famous for *Mere Christianity*.[26]

21. Alexander and McGrath, *Coming to Faith through Dawkins*.

22. Louis, "Science and Scientism," April 7, 2022, YouTube, educational video, https://www.youtube.com/watch?v=1IzPcRQ3r9A See also Plantinga, *Where the Conflict Really Lies*.

23. Hart, *Atheist Delusions*, 13–86. Hart makes a most brilliant critique of scientism in the first half of *The Experience of God*. On point, see Carkner, *Great Escape from Nihilism*.

24. Taylor, *Secular Age*, ch. 15, "The Immanent Frame," pp. 539–93.

25. Taylor, *Secular Age*.

26. Lewis, *Mere Christianity*.

He is a case in point on atheism and scientism. At a certain juncture in his journey, he came to the end of modernity's game in his mind, and mourned that it did not give him the kind of life and the higher meaning for which he longed. He was among the sharpest minds of his day, but rationalism left him feeling dead inside, without hope, revealing starkly that this kind of flat reasoning was insufficient; it did not meet his spiritual needs and aspirations (*Sehnsucht*). Reason needs faith and love to complete it. Lewis's imaginative explorations into ancient myths helped to revive his mind and his creative imagination. The CBC Radio Ideas presentation on the Inklings[27] illustrates this transition in the life and thinking of Lewis, the experience of being *surprised by joy*. A more recent coming-to-faith story of this sort can be observed in *Surprised by Oxford*[28] by Carolyn Weber. It tells a story of a young woman who found God through dialogue, wrestling, and reflection while working on her PhD in romantic literature at Oxford. It is sure to inspire those who are seekers after enchantment.

For Lewis, the result of his search led to *The Chronicles of Narnia* and his *Space Trilogy*, which refused the coldness of nihilism, materialistic naturalism, and despair (a cold, disenchanted universe). This is now some of the most celebrated literature of all time. Lewis and his friend, J. R. R. Tolkein, refused to be stifled by scientism, or broken by cynicism about human evil from two horrendous world wars. Eventually, Lewis found what he was looking for in a robust Christian faith with its commitment to compassion, fulsome reason, and a complex, fruitful humanism—rooted in the dialogue between Creation and incarnation. His universe and his imagination consequently expanded in a wonderful way that has inspired millions. He began to see where religion meets the culture spheres and animates them, where reason embraces the imagination to derive a more resilient identity, rich with higher meaning and purpose. Joseph Loconte documents the story in *A Hobbit, a Wardrobe, and a Great War: How J. R. R. Tolkien and C. S. Lewis Rediscovered Faith, Friendship, and Heroism in the Cataclysm of 1914–18.*[29] One of our speakers at the University of British Columbia in Vancouver through the Graduate and Faculty Christian Forum was Michael Ward, a theologian and Lewis literary scholar at Oxford

27. Faulk, "C. S. Lewis and the Inklings."
28. Weber, *Surprised by Oxford*.
29. Loconte, *Hobbit, a Wardrobe, and a Great War*.

University. He has written an award-winning book on *The Chronicles of Narnia* entitled *Planet Narnia*.[30]

Dialogue with God awakens us from our nihilistic, foggy, meaning-deprived slumber. It calls us away from our complacency with just getting on with the business of life, to challenge us to ask the deeper questions. It captivates us. We are strangely moved by such divine whisperings. We are awakened to great beatific announcements, revelations, epiphanies, and miracles. By addressing us in person, God calls us to become beings with a high calling: culture makers, covenant keepers, gardeners, and artisans as well as scientists, technologists, and business entrepreneurs.[31]

> God's invitations are meant to mend, shape, anchor and grow us into the character of Jesus. They call us into our true selves in Christ. They free us from the lie that says, "The more invitations the better." Invitations from the Holy One serve God's dream for the world. They don't call me to become what I produce, what others think of me or what I know. They invite me to be free. And freedom comes from being an intentional follower of Jesus—one who is a little Christ in this world.[32]

Many top scholars have broken their mind on the anvil of the incarnation and its profound implications for humanity. Theologian Jürgen Moltmann notes that "this kind of spirituality will be the restoration of a love for life, a resounding yes to life, drawing from the well of life. Vitality and liberty are linked."[33] Moral accountability and spirituality are linked in the incarnation; it is grounded in the social bonds that we share with others. Stop and listen deeply to the voice of the incarnation, divine speech writ large.

Visiting scholars have helped us to produce excellent incarnational dialogue at University of British Columbia in Vancouver, Canada in the context of the Graduate and Faculty Christian Forum. These top scholars have modeled our personal quest for incarnational spiritual culture over more than thirty years. Here are examples of our celebrated participants: Ray Aldred, Dennis Alexander, Stephen Barr, Jeremy Begbie, Francis Collins, Sy Garte, Brad Gregory, Owen Gingerich, Malcolm Guite, Deborah Haarsma, Ian Hutchinson, David Livingstone, Simon Conway Morris, Alister McGrath, Dennis Danielson, Tom McLeish, Bill Newsome, Alvin

30. Ward, *Planet Narnia*.
31. Crouch, *Culture Making*.
32. Calhoun, *Invitations from God*, 16.
33. Moltmann, *Spirit of Life*, 90.

Plantinga, Nicholas Wolterstorff, John Polkinghorne, and Jennifer Wiseman. These gifted and gracious scholars from an array of human culture spheres have made a huge impact, embodying and giving voice to the love and wisdom of Christ as they showed compatibility between their research and the biblical narrative. They have generously extended a winsome invitation to dialogue on faith and culture, with incarnation at the core. Each scholar spoke from within their field: the humanities, social sciences, hard sciences, medicine, art, literature, and music. They have modeled a profound witness for Christ and Christianity within the academy, embodying a rich combination of academic excellence and philosophical wisdom. The Graduate and Faculty Christian Forum happens to be the illustrious community from which I speak and the dialogue center that continues to inspire my reflection, teaching, and writing.

PART II. DISCERNING THE *IMAGO DEI*: GOD'S ICON

Our dialogue continues at new levels of depth. The claim by the human race to spiritual dignity and value depends on the ability to enter into an engaging, resourceful dialogue with the Creator. From the beginning of human time, mankind's task has been to mediate God's presence and glory in the world as good stewards of creation—to take responsible care of creation. This is the much-discussed *Genesis mandate*. There has unfortunately been some significant human failure over the centuries to measure up to this noble calling. In fact, the first truly successful individual to live up to the full potential of *imago Dei* was Jesus of Nazareth—the image of infinite divine being within the finite, time-space-energy-matter world. The New Testament claims that the Creator became incarnate in Jesus: The divine Word, through whom the world was made, became flesh in Jesus (John 1:3, 14). God's glory returned to Israel through this young Galilean peasant carpenter. British bishop and biblical scholar N. T. Wright writes that "Jesus at the very center of his vocation, believed himself called to do and be in relation to Israel what, in Scripture and Jewish belief, the Temple was and did."[34] As N. T. Wright explains,

> Jesus spoke and acted "as if he were the Shekinah in person, the presence of YHWH tabernacling with his people." It is now widely recognized in New Testament scholarship that against the backdrop of Second Temple Judaism, the Gospels portray Jesus as the

34. Wright, *Challenge of Jesus*, 111.

genuine temple, the definitive site of divine presence and means of connection with God.[35]

Recall that it was Jesus who said, "If you destroy this temple, I will raise it again in three days" (John 2:19). Is it any wonder that he came into conflict with the Pharisees and the Jerusalem temple authorities? Jesus is depicted by the apostles as the paradigmatic *imago Dei* (Col 1:15; Heb 1:3; 2 Cor 4:4–6). His goal was to re-enchant a broken and cynical world with a fresh vision, to remind people of the profound grace and goodness of God, to revive their sense of beauty, mystery, and wonder. He was no temporary vessel for the Word of God like one of the ancient Hebrew prophets: Elijah, Isaiah, or Jeremiah. Rather, Jesus is the man in whose human existence God willed to proceed to his final great act of revelation and redemptive self-utterance. He delivers on our human longing for transcendence and wholeness. God's grace is shown to be abundant and glorious as it reveals itself in first-century Palestine. It continues to challenge lives to this day. Jesus is the new Adam, the faithful steward of creation, the new Abraham starting a new covenant community of people who seek to mirror God's truth and goodness to one another and toward society.

Many people today sense God calling them to rethink life: to pursue and become something more challenging, noble and meaningful. They sense him calling them to move forward and upward: out of their self-pity, narcissism, and consumerism. They have tired of workaholism, resentment, anxiety, and sullenness. Before the burning bush encounter, Moses was also stuck in an aimless life, in a vocational *cul-de-sac*. Perhaps we are also called to launch a journey, innovate a solution to a major problem, make a medical breakthrough, stop a war, or follow a life-changing quest. Former Archbishop of Canterbury Rowan Williams asks insightfully, "What makes human life significant, more than animal? Not clothing, not acquisition of coverings for the naked ego, but the conscious participation in an order of compassion."[36] Love's open secret is that it offers a richer freedom and adventure in its self-giving. Love more than anything distinguishes God's kingdom people. In his thoughtful work, *The Truce of God*, Williams wants young people who have become fearful, disengaged, and alienated to turn around and take responsibility for their world as peacemakers, community builders, healers, and servant-leaders. They can discover the motivation to do this in Christ. Incarnational spiritual culture is a very real turnaround

35. Middleton, "New Earth Perspective," 83.

36. Williams, *Truce of God*, 96.

story. It involves former egocentrics, prodigals, and cynics in just treatment of the poor, widows, and orphans. This is Jesus's legacy as *imago Dei* for a new world with palpable promise and hope (Matt 25).

Our contemporary Athens is sensate, hedonistic, and materialistic. But innovative ideas emerge when we break free of self-defeating behavior, become vulnerable and engage life in good faith, as we join with others in community. To love is to renounce the quest of being an island, of keeping one's options constantly open through radical self-interest. Late modern author Andy Crouch discusses this important search for wisdom: "Making sense of the wonder and the terror of the world is the original human preoccupation. And it is the deepest sense of culture that most clearly distinguishes us from all the rest of creation."[37] We dearly long for the articulate grasp, this capacity to make sense of our experience and relationships. At our deepest and happiest core, we humans are meaning-makers, stewards, purpose-driven contributors. Terrorism, fear, violence, fate, oppression, and murder do not have the last word. Long-term battles are won by good ideas that include alternative strategies, the right vision, and fresh eyes of interpretation. New creativity and confidence emerge with fresh art, new ways of perceiving, and contributing to the common good. Without such vision, people shrink back and perish. That is the unprecedented power of the Christ: God's glory and grace shines forth from the obedient Word of God in the crucified and resurrected rabbi, Jesus of Nazareth. He lives out most fully the vocation of image of God, making him an excellent example. Incarnation is primarily grounded in the nature of God, not the nature of humanity. It is God's invitation. Jesus is divine holiness revealed in the course of a human biography. He allows the character of God to shine forth dramatically through his life and teaching.

Incarnation presents humanity with the possibility of full, but finite, personal embodiment of *Logos*, the will and wisdom of the divine. As a fleshly, personal wisdom, it sets out an alternative paradigm from self-mastery, self-invention, and self-promotion. Jesus is the image (icon) of God that we long for in our honest moments, the most excellent representative of God on earth. He interprets, makes sense of us and our addicted and broken world. He is fully God and fully engaged human. In this way, he provides an excellent model of life lived in the presence of God, offering us an *archetype* of human goodness that is inspired directly from heaven. Jesus is a phenomenal gift to us. Duke University theologian D. Stephen

37. Crouch, *Culture Making*, 24.

Long appeals to the *moral normativity* of the life of Jesus, revealing that we humans are hard-wired for such a transcendent-immanent, I-Thou relationship.

> In Christian theology, Jesus reveals to us not only who God is but also what it means to be *truly human*. This true humanity is not something we achieve on our own; it comes to us as a gift. . . . The reception of this gift contains an ineliminable element of mystery that will always require faith. Jesus in his life, teaching, death and resurrection and ongoing presence in the church and through the Holy Spirit . . . orders us towards God. He directs our passions and desires towards that which can finally fulfill them and bring us happiness.[38]

There is both reason and romance, thought and artfulness in the Jesus story. Over against otherworldly Gnosticism, transcendent goodness is made present and accessible in the human sphere, in *embodied* existence, through the incarnation of God in Jesus. This is definitely something new in history. It offers us a *transcendent turn* to a new kind of humanism centered in *agape* love. Transcendence of the *strong* variety[39] does not mean apathy, aloofness or indifference. Nor is it a burdensome or unreachable abstract standard of perfectionism. Neither is it merely a Kantian moral imperative. Rather, it is a creative, palpable engagement with the world—with nature, individuals, society, public institutions, and politics. Jesus shows that this goodness can be thought, related to, and lived out freely and robustly within the human theater. He mirrors grace, holiness, truth, and mercy.[40] The final litmus test or plausibility of a good moral philosophy is its applicability, livability, its real-world *praxis*. This renders it both credible and desirable. Christ is complete and distinct in his humanity, while still remaining God. This leaves us in awe.

Jesus provides an interpretive lens of what God wants from us, with great prospects for change for the human imagination. Although this claim is challenging, Paul the apostle in Col 1:15–20 speaks of Jesus as the source and bond of creation, as well as the purpose and end (*telos*) of creation. He is both its creative *alpha* and *omega*, its origin and final trajectory. He is *above all things* in creation and at the same time the creative basis, the very ground of being. He is that without which nothing would exist, without which this

38. Long, *Goodness of God*, 106–7.

39. Schrag, *Self after Postmodernity*, 110.

40. This theme is extended in chapter 5.

very text would be meaningless gibberish. The fullness of God dwells in him. He is God incarnate, fully God and fully man, as the Athanasian tradition states. In him, God's eternity connects with creation's temporality. Paul captures its power when he encourages the Corinthian church, "Jesus is the Yes and Amen to it all" (2 Cor 1:18–21, my paraphrase). He identifies with the human condition while setting out a new *social imaginary* for moral, spiritual, and identity capacity. He is for justice, mutual accountability, both within one's individual life and within one's social identity. Jesus as a model of the *imago Dei* enriches us, fills us with unconquerable hope for a better world. He strengthens our very mental health and human consciousness—responsibility and justice for the other. He animates noble spiritual desires within us. Theologically, Jesus Christ is the human being who is the Second Person of the Trinity—the Word and the Son of the Father. This Word has two natures: human and divine, one of which is his as eternally divine, never to be diminished. His humanity is fully constituted with body, will, emotions, memory, capacity for love, and intellect—full personhood.

In his very thoughtful doctoral dissertation on the *imago Dei*, biblical scholar J. Richard Middleton claims in *The Liberating Image*[41] that Jesus accomplishes all that was anticipated in humans to become as a proper representative of God's character on earth. He faithfully fulfilled the Genesis mandate as mediator of God's presence and goodness. Jesus depicts the complete human, a high caliber of humanity. He is the critical *nexus* of the eternal and the temporal, the transcendent and the immanent. He is a powerful exemplar of divine love, redirecting our passions , showing us the way to live humbly, hospitably, and justly. Inspired by Jesus's life and teaching, individuals do not need to deny or fear their desire for God-dialogue. Rather, Jesus encourages this dialogue, this close friendship with God. One implication of the incarnation is that Christianity offers participation in the very life of God. He succeeded regarding the mission of *imago Dei* where many others in the biblical narrative failed. It was a costly journey of obedience and covenant faithfulness to his Father's will. For Jesus, everything is God-bathed, full of wonder; it is all about God's will, honor, and glory.

Incarnation bestows a tremendous gift of grace which dignifies human existence. Offering us a more robust identity and higher purpose, he came to take us forward both morally and spiritually. In conversation and relationship with him, we step out of the shadows of our lies, lust for power, and deceptions, and into the light—the holiness, joy, and delight that is

41. Middleton, *Liberating Image*.

God (2 Pet 1:4). In *Scandal*, the popular fictional television series, Olivia Pope, also known as *the fixer*, is hired to save people's reputation in the halls of power in Washington. She is very highly skilled at her job. But she sees so much darkness that, at times, she longs to leave it all, quit the job, and step out of the shadows into the light. She becomes tired of spinning the truth, making excuses for bad behavior. She is paid to get powerful people off the hook for evil they have committed, exploitative actions or damaging words. Jesus incarnates the deep reason for this human longing for noble character, moral clarity, and genuine virtue. He helps us understand that we are the accountable *moral animal*. Integrity matters. Justice matters. Mercy matters. He is the ultimate reason for doing the right thing, even if it is not easy or convenient. Regardless of our context and our past failures, the inspirational goal set by Jesus's life is to remain faithful to one's highest convictions, covenants, and principles. Remember that a disenchanted world is often a boring one because it leaves us slothful, restless, irritable, and prone to corruption.

German theologian, Dietrich Bonhoeffer, was a Christian humanist who believed strongly in the incarnational lifestyle during the Second World War under the terror of fascism in Germany. He felt called to the heroic life and thus he returned to Germany from a comfortable teaching job in America at Union Seminary. He formed part of the resistance to the Nazi regime, and through his seminary, he tried to shore up Christian faith among German believers. This involved what was then called the *Confessing Church*. He rightly regarded full, costly, moral humanity as the ultimate goal of God's work in Christ.[42] This conviction gave him the fortitude and courage to resist evil with his whole being—to put his life on the line. Bonhoeffer learned firsthand about the costly grace and deep joy that this would entail. He was arrested, interrogated, and sadly hung just before the war ended. Much was lost, but so much more was gained for the kingdom of God. He was faithful to his convictions to his last breath as an incarnational disciple of Jesus. He remains an inspiring, consequential model of the *imago Dei*, of Christian faithfulness. His faith, fueled by knowing and loving God, kept him resilient even while in prison and under interrogation. His legacy speaks volumes to our current ambivalent human condition. We too can find this quality of call as *imago Dei*, mediating God's presence and glory to promote *shalom* in society. It increases our capacity

---

42. Zimmermann, *Dietrich Bonhoeffer's Christian Humanism*.

for good, meaning a life well-invested, or what Yale theologian Miraslof Volf calls *human flourishing*.[43]

Further reading on this rich and powerful theme of Jesus as the *imago Dei* can be found in Darrell Johnson's pithy work *Who Is Jesus?* I remember encountering this enlightening connection in a three-part sermon series a few years ago. He did a masterful job of linking Jesus's life and witness to Old Testament expectations for the Son of Man, Son of God, Suffering Servant, and Lamb of God themes. Johnson points out that one of the characteristic terms used for Jesus in the New Testament is the *Son of Man*. It appears some eighty times.

> The Son of Man reminded first century people of a special figure in the drama of God's salvation of the world. In the seventh chapter of his book, the prophet Daniel tells of a vision God gave him one night, a vision affecting the course of world history. . . . All peoples, nations and language groups serve this [person]. He is the universal figure worthy of universal worship. . . . Jesus was claiming to be that towering figure of Daniel's vision. . . . As the Son of Man, Jesus the Christ has the authority to execute judgment.[44]

The use of this term was part of what got Jesus into trouble with the Jewish authorities who considered it blasphemous—meaning that he claimed to be God although appearing to them merely human. This was interpreted as self-idolatry, a crime in that culture. Because of this, they believed that they must eliminate him as a false Messianic claimant. It all turns on whether we can accept him as God's Savior or not. When we begin to see the world the way Jesus sees it, it also shocks our perception of ourselves. Philosopher Paul Gould writes concerning this position:

> By perceiving the world as enchanted, we savor it, and find sustenance in it. . . . The path of return to God [to enchantment] lies through creation itself. We can't return to this God-infused reality by denying or devaluing the material world. All that God made is good. All is intrinsically valuable and sacred, even as it is broken and bent. . . . Creation is *haunted*. Creation ushers us into God's presence as we learn to see God in and through all he has made.[45]

That includes the Jewish virgin Mary who gave birth to his Son. How are we to live up to the fullness of *imago Dei*? It is challenging to fathom the

43. Volf, *Flourishing*.

44. Johnson, *Who Is Jesus?*, 45–48.

45. Gould, *Cultural Apologetics*, 83.

concept of the *infinite within the finite*. The eternal Son assumed human nature. Jesus is both human and divine, not by converting Godhead into flesh, but by taking manhood into God.

Our discussion now leaves us in a good place to proceed to chapter 3 on Jesus as the Ground of Wisdom. This is at the heart of the matter. We have now entered a discourse full of wonder and possibility, a clarion call. This has been a foundational chapter on the subject of dialogue with God and discovery of our fundamental calling by the incarnation of Christ Jesus, the shining exemplum of *imago Dei*. It makes a huge difference where we ground our identity, and we have discovered that our identity is irreducibly dialogical (Gal 2:20). It is received from God, not achieved by us. It is a gift within a relationship; our calling to mirror God has been restored through the incarnation. We ultimately want to arrive at full coherence in our worldview, living a robust life, including the practical dimensions. Lives are transformed by this encounter; there are new levels of understanding and experience to discover ahead.

3

Jesus the Ground of Wisdom

PART I. THE INCARNATE WISDOM OF GOD IN CHRIST

Wisdom is a vital language that we need to recover today. Our world can be confusing, even overwhelming with the current speed of change.[1] We are going through revolutions in biotech (Epigenetics), and infotech (Artificial Intelligence and Quantum Computing). Added to this, we face worldwide pandemics (COVID), nuclear and climate threats. The clash of superpowers hoping for world domination is regularly in the news (Russia, China, and America). We corporately need discernment and a high level of wisdom in order to traverse such an age, to negotiate our differences and tensions. Questions arise: Who do we trust in good faith and how do we work together peacefully and constructively? Whom can we count on for the truth, for good and inclusive governing policy? How do we solve these intractable global problems while paying attention to the marginalized? Where is sound leadership to be found? What influences are shaping our next generation leaders? Where are they to find good, sound, and wise mentors?

The New Testament makes the amazing claims that Jesus is, in the flesh, *the wisdom of God and the power of God* (1 Cor 1:24). He is the *nexus* of knowledge and ethics, integral to the relationship between faith and reason. As the divine *Logos* (John 1:1–4), he is the transcendent Word made flesh,

1. Harari, *21 Lessons for the 21st Century.*

plus the underwriter of all human thought and language. Truth ultimately is found embodied in a person of highest credibility, not a mere philosophy or ideology. Jesus is deep reason personified, the *raison d'être* of it all. The narrative is clear: The incarnation is a *communicative action*,[2] a *theodrama*, not just letters, propositions, or sentences. The Jesus story is wisdom writ large, saturated with insight that offers a foundation for addressing our past, present, and future. Can the incarnation form the basis for reconciliation, confront lies and violence, bring peace and heal divisions? As we proceed, we long to explore the depths of this proposition.

Christians believe that all truth points to its source in Christ, the Creator of all things in the cosmos. We arrive at the truth when our thoughts, beliefs and statements correspond to reality, when we are properly related to the world as it is—*critical realism*. Therefore, faithfulness to Christ requires diligent cultivation of the intellectual virtues.[3] Christians ought not to be anti-intellectual, because the pursuit of knowledge is valuable in its own right. It reveals more about God and the wonder and complexity of his world. I have enjoyed many great mentors who have brought me closer to a more disciplined understanding of the truth. They inspired me with a hunger for acute knowledge and cogent insight. Our faith and beliefs should not be based on myth, scam, or hearsay, but critical biblical, scientific, and historical thinking.[4] We are more secure in our beliefs when they have been tested as in our debates with culture (1 Pet 3:15). I have always been a strong advocate of honest and robust Christian apologetics and engaging dialogue in my campus career.[5] This is important because our beliefs matter deeply—they are the very rails on which our life travels. In biblical theism, mind is prior to, or transcends and causes, matter or body. Philosopher Paul Gould speaks to the logic of hard thinking and rigorous investigation.

> We would expect a perfectly rational and good personal being to spread his joy and delight by creating a world full of epistemic, moral, and aesthetic value. For in such a world it is possible to

---

2. Vanhoozer, *Is There a Meaning?*

3. Zagzebski, *Virtues of the Mind*.

4. Watkin, *Critical Biblical Theory*.

5. Among my favorites: Norman Geisler, Alvin Plantinga, James Sire, William Lane Craig, Brian Walsh, C. Steven Evans, Rebecca McLaughlin, James K. A. Smith, and Charles Taylor.

love, know, act, and create. It is easy to see how such features could
be exhibited in a world created by a personal God.[6]

Gould captures the fuller breadth of Christian reflection (science, ethics,
the arts) answering the tough questions put to the faith. It makes a vast
difference if we are in a world governed by truth and not mere survival
instincts. Truth should not be bent to our will or self-interest. The reasoning process is deliberative. It involves various components as we examine
the plausibility and cogency of Christianity: (a) the reception of facts from
sensation, reports of others (i.e., testimony that includes history), memory,
introspection, or the imagination; (b) the perception of self-evident truths,
including laws of logical inference; (c) the arrangement of facts to arrive at
new truths that are not so self-evident; (d) the discernment or interpretation of claims and reports of third parties to sort the credible from the falla-
cious, the robust from the shallow claims (hermeneutics); (e) the search for
evidence of God's artwork in creation (science and philosophy of science).
Cambridge theology professor Andrew Davison agrees. Metaphysical realism means that "something objective underlies any true sense of things,
whether in knowledge of a creature or in a creature's witness to God. It
does not however require a denial of contingency or mediation. . . . At root,
knowledge is a witness to reality, based on a reception from that reality."[7]
Human rationality is not simply logic-crunching or data mining; it is also
deeply integrated with hopes, desires, intentions, and emotions

Jesus is God's truest and highest revelation on earth, located and embodied truth, claiming that "If you hold to my teaching, you are really my
disciples. Then you will know the truth, and the truth will set you free"
(John 8:31–2). Teachability, humility, and freedom embrace one another in
the truth and wisdom quest. Jesus is *public truth*, so he is not to be brushed
aside lightly. He and his life teachings are to be seriously reckoned with in
the marketplace of ideas. His words have had a profound impact throughout the last twenty centuries and continue to do so worldwide. In one of my
blog posts, I reflect on this point and why truth is important to Christian
identity.[8] There is a palpable power in these words of Jesus. We will need to
lean into them if we are to fathom their impact for our life journey. Jesus is
the way of wisdom, the way of deep structure integrity and personal wholeness, the way of life-giving *agape* love. He is the *sign* of something more to

6. Gould, *Cultural Apologetics*, 131.

7. Davison, *Astrobiology and Christian Doctrine*, 119.

8. Carkner, "What is Truth and Why Does it Matter?"

the world, the *signifier* of God's great interest in mankind, and the *signified* as the meaning and goal of all history. Jesus is also part of the very inner life and communion of God the Trinity—the center and source of all reality. Musician Kari Jobe captures something of the breadth and complexity of this insight in her beautiful song *Forever*. A very fruitful, life-changing conversation awaits those curious about the suffering servant who died for our sins, broke the back of evil, and who is now the resurrected God-man ascended to the Father's right hand. Jesus's life and teaching delivers immense, culture-shaping ramifications that rattle the rafters of the house of thought—of academia as well as everyday life and commerce. Christopher Watkin is absolutely brilliant in demonstrating this in his award-winning book that rigorously engages the biblical narrative with contemporary culture (early and late modernity): *Biblical Critical Theory*.[9]

Biblically, we are called and invited to seek wisdom, build our lives on it—the Psalms and Proverbs. Dare we allow it to take our minds captive to Jesus's Lordship, his sovereign care (2 Cor 10)? We are called to change the way we think and perceive reality—our entire world and life view, our *social imaginary*, is at stake. In other words, we need his oversight, and his scrutiny as we think hard, act astutely, and pursue noble character which includes the virtues as a lifelong pursuit. He is intensely interested in our new ideas and thoughts for a more just, peaceful, and fair world. It is one with less violence and injustice, more compassion and inclusion. He can help us bring these dreams to fruition, because they are grounded in God's will and wisdom.

Jesus is the *omega point* of wisdom, the ultimate fulfillment of every human spiritual, religious, moral, and philosophical aspiration. This is a high claim that runs through the whole New Testament discourse. For example, the apostle Paul claims this as he opens a dialogue with the Greek philosophers at the Areopagus in Acts chapter 17. He engages them through their own poets and philosophers. He shows them that they, in their depths, actually long for what Jesus offers. To the point, it is incarnation that shows that Jesus has healed the broken semiotic relationship between *word* and *world*,[10] an alienation that is endemic to late modernity. Imagine the Creator of billions of galaxies, all mountains, landscapes, and oceans and all peoples. That same divine being has come to live among us as a member of the human race, taking a serious interest in us and our

9. Watkin, *Biblical Critical Theory*.

10. Hunter, *To Change the World*.

problems personally. He is available for scrutiny, subject to examination by people of every belief persuasion, every tribe, every form of skepticism or agnosticism. He provides the chance to make sense of life. Jesus is the *shalom* of God in the flesh, full *presence*, providing for us a way to peace and a new fruitfulness of existence. He offers the energy, momentum, and purpose that we crave. He takes us beyond mere animal survival toward abundant flourishing. When Paul asks us to *ground our identity in Christ* in his letters to the Ephesians and Colossians, he is deeply serious that this is the way out of our current existential identity crisis.[11]

Wisdom shows up as an Old Testament (the Hebrew Bible) personification in Proverbs chapter 8. Lady wisdom provides a framework and a profound motivation for our thinking, reflection, and ultimate discernment. She addresses some of the perennial problems we face: grinding poverty, inequity, oppression, governmental and business corruption, insatiable greed, pride, and entitlement. We all know that we need fresh wisdom in our institutions today, as a book by Professor Eugene Soltes reveals.[12] It was made public by investigators that the opioid epidemic had a lot to do with corporate greed and a tragic loss of moral compass. Jesus as personal, divine-human wisdom today cries out like a prophet to late moderns in the public squares of our towns and globalized mega-cities: Come to me, and learn from me. Experience my sanity, realism, and joy. Let's talk about the constructive way forward, the way to avoid the nightmare scenario—the various cultural death spirals. Let's talk about your paralyzing anger, shame, and fear. Let me teach you servant leadership, how to patiently suffer with others, to show hospitality, to see yourself in the needs of others. Let me help you discern and grapple with your joyous responsibility for the common good, learn how to help the marginalized, and stop the violence.

Our minds and hearts are challenged at the highest level by Jesus. There is a sense in which he draws into focus all the words of the Old and New Testaments. He is the *apogee*, the fulfillment of all the promises made to the ancient Hebrew patriarchs (Abraham, Isaac, Israel, etcetera). He is the leading edge of the prophetic utterances; he speaks and teaches from within the wisdom tradition. The spiritual longings of the ancient wise ones for this Son of Man redeemer, the Jewish Messiah, are fulfilled in him. The promise doctrine, woven into the whole biblical narrative over

11. Peterson, *Practice Resurrection*.

12. Soltes, *Why They Do It*.

centuries, is fulfilled in him.[13] The evidence is in the promise of redemption, renewal, and justice for the poor.[14] Humans have spent much time anticipating someone who could show a better way to conduct politics and economics, someone who would promote human dignity, one who would protect the innocent, the weak, and the marginalized. We see this in his hard but very good teaching in The Sermon on the Mount (Matt 5–7). An answer to many prayers, Jesus entered this world to save us from our own destructive violence and vengeance, our foolishness, while teaching us the higher wisdom of God (Jas 3:13–18). His life constitutes a unique story, a powerful narrative of restoration and renewal, of resurrection and hope for a better future. It circulates throughout the world today as the brilliant apex of God's redemptive initiatives.

People need not suffer from hopelessness: a shallow, purposeless existence of either grinding survival or selfish entitlement. They need not give up their freedom of thought and speech, reason or identity to some ideology: like stripped-down materialism, manipulative determinism, deconstructionism, or populism. Nor do they need to give into addictions to social media, video games, or tribalistic propaganda wars of the political right or left. Instead, individuals can begin to embrace life on a higher plain beyond their own self-interest and prejudice. They will discover that they were created to serve others and glorify God—the highest purpose. They become creative, live a richer lifestyle of benevolence and joy. Regent College philosophical theologian Jens Zimmermann's summary insight on this point offers a fresh articulation of reality within the biblical template of wisdom. Jesus lived no ordinary life; he was not just another rabbi or guru looking for a group of sycophants. He instead is a sure anchor in the storms of life, a strong source of hope in the midst of despair.

> Christ the creative wisdom of God, and God's active Word in creation, is enfleshed in the temporal-historical dimension of our world as the concrete Jewish Messiah, Jesus the Christ. . . . This is the Word through whom all things were made, and the Word hid in the eternal bosom of God, the Word who spoke through the prophets, the Word whose mighty acts defined the history of Israel. In Jesus the Christ this Word has become flesh, and the eternal has become temporal, but without ceasing to be eternal. . . . In Christ temporality and eternity are conjoined. . . . In the incarnation, creation, the world, time and history have been taken up into

13. Kaiser, *Promise Plan of God.*

14. Peterson, *Jesus Way.*

the God-man, who *is* the center of reality. . . . Faith and reason are inseparable because their unity is in Christ.[15]

This is a very powerful, comprehensive statement. Divine poetic language or *speech act* (John Searle) starts with creation: God spoke and the heavens, the stars, the seas, the plants and trees, living creatures, man and woman came into being. Amanda Cook brings this powerfully to life in her song "So Will I (100 Billion X)." Motivated by love, Jesus the Son was there with the Father and the Holy Spirit at creation's dawn, calling forth all things into fruitful existence through his wisdom. He is the creative source of all human life, of the moral good and justice, of imagination and artistic expression, of calling and stewardship. Divine speech continues in Jesus as the true, faithful, and obedient Son of God on earth. As divine *Logos*, he provides the very architecture of creation. He is the incarnational logic of creation (Col 1:15–20). Biology and meta-biology (science and meaning) are made whole in Christ, who is the ultimate hermeneutic. The designative (scientific) and constitutive (religious) languages, articulated by Charles Taylor in *The Language Animal*, work together as they grasp reality: material, moral, spiritual, historical.[16] Articulacy is critical for Taylor, Canada's greatest philosopher. Constitutive language can open new spaces for human meanings and identity: new terms, new expressions, enactments, new fields of articulacy. Thus he warns, "The scientific zone can only be a suburb of the vast, sprawling city of language, and could never be the metropolis itself."[17] Christ identifies with us as language animals who want more, who seek higher meaning, deeper satisfaction, inspiring spirituality, purpose, and wholeness.

This insight on wisdom urges that we look beyond mere human flourishing in terms of safety and self-interest. We are called to look towards the fullest benefit to mankind, our fullest human dignity—a *thick*, responsible self within a lively community (chapter 4). We want to negotiate a whole landscape of meaning. We need to dig deep in enactments, articulation, and reflection and be open to higher aspirations regarding our goals, calling, and skill set. In the birth, life, teaching, sacrificial death, resurrection, and ascension of Jesus the Christ, we are offered nothing short of a new design for human society where the strong work with the handicapped to level the playing field—mutual flourishing. His life and teachings represent

15. Zimmerman, *Incarnational Humanism*, 264–65.
16. Taylor, *Language Animal*, esp. chs. 6 and 7, pp. 177–288.
17. Taylor, *Language Animal*, 263.

an inspiration—a gripping and tantalizing call to a larger life, a stronger identity with redemptive and healing impact. Moreover, this richer life is a journey forward in moral-spiritual-identity growth: with results in seeing better, thinking more clearly, living closer to the very force of life. Jesus the Word of God is a symbol of a whole new relationship between humanity and the cosmos, bringing God's loving yet unsettling presence and power among us to redeem us. It poses many questions that demand our attention, pushing out the bounds of what it means to be human, possibly beyond our comfort zone, but also for our good. This move raises the bar to expand our identity far beyond the reductionistic grip of the *immanent frame*.[18] Notwithstanding, it is also extremely relevant to the practical issues of everyday social and political life—raising children, sorting out disputes, voting, and responsible government. University of West Georgia history professor Daniel K. Williams writes about these implications in *The Politics of the Cross*.[19] He addresses this incarnational, suffering servant perspective on citizenship and governance.

One major implication of the wisdom articulated in the incarnation is that Christianity is no mere religion to placate the gods, including the god of self-idolatry. It involves us in participation in the very life of God; it includes an amazing friendship and communion with a holy God as Trinity: Father, Son and Holy Spirit. This *presence* of God in Christ makes him the ideal human image bearer,[20] mediating heaven's will to earthlings. He clears a path and draws us toward our full humanization. Others before Jesus, including Israel as a nation, have tried to measure up to the noble, kingly and priestly calling of *imago Dei*. The incarnation (John 1:1–5, 14; Col 1:15–20) provides a vision to restore late modern broken relationships such as racism, radical economic inequality, and corruption of power interests. It is a different foundation for reality, a thorough critique of culture. He can heal us from fragmentation and disenchantment, bring us back from the abyss of hypocrisy and disingenuous power games. It is in this world, this neighborhood, this city that Christ offers unequivocal change for the better.[21] Our apologetic for wisdom combines reason with experience, historicity with existential impact, the arts with science.[22]

18. Taylor, *Secular Age*, 539–93.
19. Williams, *Politics of the Cross*.
20. Middleton, *Liberating Image*.
21. Wallis, *(Un)Common Good*.
22. McLeish, *Faith and Wisdom in Science*.

Both Christ himself, and the church which he left behind upon his ascension, are an incarnation. At their most authentic, they act out a *faithful presence*[23] that represents God's intent for society. This conviction involves an important union of Christology and Pneumatology (Jesus and the Holy Spirit) which will be explained in more detail in both chapters 4 and 5. We find it in the apostle John's discourse in the book of John, chapters 14–17. It is the unity of Christ-Spirit and the church, a beautiful interface: always working together as part of the Trinity. Redemption through Christ blossoms into harmonious social communion. It abandons extreme individualism, but without dismissing the importance of the creative, entrepreneurial individual to build a better future. To summarize our thought thus far, we find a powerful covenant relationship articulated in a vision statement from University of Virginia's reputable sociologist James Davison Hunter:

> I have argued that there is a different foundation for reality and thus a different kind of binding commitment symbolized most powerfully in the incarnation. The incarnation represents an alternative way by which word and world come together. It is in the incarnation and the particular way the Word became incarnate in Jesus Christ that we find the only adequate reply to the challenges of dissolution and difference. If, indeed, there is a hope or an imaginable prospect for human flourishing in the contemporary world, it begins when the Word of *shalom* becomes flesh in us and is enacted through us toward those with whom we live, in the tasks we are given, and in the spheres of influence in which we operate. When the Word of all flourishing—defined by the love of Christ— becomes flesh in us, in our relations with others, within the tasks we are given, and within our spheres of influence—absence gives way to presence, and the word we speak to each other and to the world becomes authentic and trustworthy. This is the heart of the theology of faithful presence.[24]

The impact is that one becomes a unique person with a distinct role and responsibility to play out in the community's effort to transform the entire culture (Rom 8). One builds stewardship of creation and society into one's intimate life experiences. This individual human uniqueness is rooted in the absolute uniqueness of God in Christ. "In redeeming the created order, Christ redeems social relationships among creatures, relationships

23. Hunter, *To Change the World*, 237–54.

24. Hunter, *To Change the World*, 252. See his beautiful elaboration of this concept (pp. 238–51).

that are intrinsic to created human nature."[25] He came to heal and unify humanity, to heal fragmented, polarized people into a community of mutuality. This is the foundation of contemporary human rights discourse. The incarnation affirms and elevates the whole human race in their fullest dimensionality. *Theodrama*, according to Swiss theologian Hans Urs von Balthasar, says this:

> The audience's nonneutral, contemplative awareness forms a "communion" between the author's (God the Father) vision, the actor's (Jesus the Christ) visible embodiment of the vision on stage and the audience's (human) cooperation in the presentation of the vision. The audience is invited on stage into this *theodrama* by the Holy Spirit to participate in the play, thus opening themselves to being enraptured by the divine mystery revealed in Christ's incarnation.[26]

The drama of the incarnate Word unfolds wonderfully in the life of the church and beyond, to transform social institutions. The witness of the Holy Spirit is also a key component of the incarnation that we address more fully in chapter 5. The closer one comes to the Son, following his call, the more unique, free, and mentally healthy one can become. "The notion of emptying oneself in love characterizes Balthasar's view of reality, from the relations within the Trinity, through creation, incarnation and saving work of Christ, onto the expected response of the creature in self-giving love."[27] This outstanding love of God encounters humanity in understandable and practical terms, instituting a whole new economy of grace—God reaching out to the disenchanted through Christ's followers.

As we have shown, Jesus takes an interest in us, addressing each human being individually, awakening us spiritually, and calling us to our higher self. Therefore, each must decide if they will seek to embody this wisdom in turn, and bear the name of Christ with dignity. Will you accept the unique, powerful mission God has for you? It is only by identifying with this mission that humans become full persons in the deepest existential and theological sense. This produces an ongoing transformation of self as an embodied person, embedded fruitfully within society. Personhood is not dissolved, stunted, or muted when one decides to follow Jesus. Rather, it is enhanced as we enter the dialogue, receive the word, and partake in the

25. Mongrain, *Systematic Thought of Balthasar*, 199.

26. Mongrain, *Systematic Thought of Balthasar*, 201.

27. Gawronski, *Word and Silence*, 163.

drama. We become articulate world stewards and culture makers.[28] We see and are seen, know and are known. God's great work of art in the incarnation inspires people to become players: creative artists, stewardly gardeners, teachers of truth who cultivate and mentor virtues into healthy lives. There is an unfathomable depth to Jesus's wisdom that leads to a lifestyle that shows word and deed as a coherence. If you want to take your faith to the next level, read on.

PART II. SIX PILLARS OF INCARNATIONAL WISDOM FROM HANS URS VON BALTHASAR.

Balthasar has a strong articulate grasp when it comes to the incarnation and its larger frame, its broader horizon of meaning. God can be known in diverse but commensurable ways by different cultures and peoples. I have elaborated below six of his critical observations.

1. **Positive Revelation:** A philosophically derived negative theology (*via negativa*) must not be allowed to supplant the positive revelation of the supernatural mystery in Christ.[29] This is to distinguish *mystery* from the *mysticism* of the *un-word* (Zen). The incarnation is the deepest, richest and most permanent source of infinite, divine mystery offered within the finite order. It assumes that the transcendent Creator God of Jewish monotheism is the same God who became fully incarnate in Jesus of Nazareth. Jesus and Christianity represents a renewed monotheism in a Trinitarian mode. Humans have no more at hand, fuller, and clearer access to the Creator than in Christ. We know this by reflection on the Christ events of history rather than mere *speculation*. Historical particularity is vital to incarnation. Jesus is not an avatar. Christopher Watkin writes, "God enters history at a particular moment to gather a people to be with him, not in a Greek eternity of unchanging timelessness, but in a biblical eternity of never-ending and ever renewed intimacy and relational richness."[30]

2. **Existential Hermeneutic:** Incarnation means that theologians and pastoral leaders must allow God's self-revelation in Jesus Christ to interpret itself in the lives of believers through the work of the Holy

---

28. Crouch, *Culture Making.*
29. Gawronski, *Word and Silence*, 75–132.
30. Watkin, *Biblical Critical Theory*, 367.

Spirit and spiritual guidance within the church. They must be spiritually formed as *Christ-ones*. This includes the art of spiritual formation. In Jesus, we see revealed the holiness of a transparent life of sacrificial love (justice, mercy, and humility), and this is the character of life we in turn are to model. This touches on the area of theological anthropology. Balthasar is against abstract, modern reinterpretations or epic views such as those found in the works of German philosopher G. F. W. Hegel, well-known for his idealism. The problem of epic theology is that God tends to be either absorbed into the cosmos (pantheism), or else he is totally banished from it (atheism/exclusive humanism/scientism) in ideologies such as neo-Marxism or Libertarianism. For both modernity and postmodernity, also known as early and late modernity, abstract structure is taken as more fundamental than the particular—the existential life lived. But it is unnecessary and unhelpful to elevate the abstract universal at the expense of the concrete particular. Aberrations from the incarnation paradigm always entail reductionism of full personhood, some retreat from wholistic and authentic particularity. This often leads to oppression and violence, forcing persons into the mold of some ideology or cultic following of a populist guru. This is why the Gospels are so vital in depicting the life and teaching of Jesus—exemplifying how we are to live and love robustly, faithfully.

3. **Transcendence and Immanence:** Christian theology must always discern that the eternal divine realm and temporal created realm are separated by a large ontological gap. That gap is bridged, but not erased, by Christ's overall mission of redemption.[31] The transcendent and immanent remain intact with the incarnation. "In Jesus, we find the Person of the Word with two natures, human and divine, one intrinsically his as eternally Divine, the other assumed 'for us' and our salvation."[32] Christ is both complete human (body, soul, will, memory, and intellect) and yet distinct in his humanity—the Word does not change, is not reduced. This is something really new and profound, a whole new intimate relationship with humanity. Judeo-Christianity remains one integrated salvation narrative in four acts: Creation, Fall, Incarnation, and Redemption. The incarnate Word interprets himself within historical time while possessing an ongoing link to eternity.

31. Mongrain, *Systematic Thought of Balthasar*, 204.

32. Davison, *Astrobiology and Christian Doctrine*, 251.

Incarnational theology and spirituality are focused on both the temporal and eternal. William T. Cavanaugh captures it: "What makes the form of Christ attractive is the perfect harmony between finite form and infinite fullness, the particular and the universal."[33] God, creation, and humans are all seen to be key players in this greater heaven-earth kingdom drama. Consequently, we draw on theology, science, and anthropology as interwoven themes within the incarnation social imaginary.

4. **Incarnation Entails a Sense of Wonder:**[34] The allure of Christ leads us to experience the ever-greater mystery of God. We get fresh insight into the divine. The glory and wonder of the story of Christ continues to open up both transcendent and immanent reality to us. Jesus is the enticing window into the divine that opens the potential to both be *known by*, and to *know* God. Jesus *is* the living Gospel of God approaching us and calling us, offering friendship. He often said in the Gospels, "I am He," meaning YHWH (God in the flesh), God among you.[35] Unlike religious-cultural systems in which the word is uttered out of silence, the divine Word in Christian faith is uttered from the eternal fullness of the Father, and the incarnation speaks from out of the fullness of the *perichoretic* communion within Trinitarian life. Amidst fragmented and confusing human utterance, Jesus articulates the speech of God to humankind, and through his mediation and prayers, human needs to God. This sets up profound human-divine dialogue with existential impact. Thus, incarnation reveals the love, wisdom, and artfulness of God.

5. **Orthodoxy Combines with Orthopraxis:** On the theme of the Word-Deed, the unity of creation and redemption, the synthesis of faith and love, contemplation and action demonstrates that faith is meant to be lived both intellectually and through compassionate actions or *praxis*. Contemplation alone is not sufficient to complete and authenticate faith. Doctrinal teaching and ethics (including integration of the virtues), are a critical combination to make the believer whole spiritually—an integrated follower. Truth has this kind of layered depth. We find this beautiful balance in Paul's letter to the Philippians chapter

33. Cavanaugh, *Being Consumed*, 79.

34. Mongrain, *Systematic Thought of Balthasar*, 204.

35. Johnson, *Who Is Jesus?*, 94–111. YHWH (LORD) is the Hebrew covenant name of God.

2:12–13: "Continue to work out your salvation with fear and trembling, for it is God who works in you to will and to act in order to fulfill his good purpose." He always includes in each of his letters to young churches one or more chapters on how believers are to live the gospel of the kingdom sociologically. This includes the impact of love within the context of Christian community and outward to the world at large.

6. **Church Social Practice and *Agape* Miracles:** Rooted in the unity of Christ and the church, any legitimate Christian theology and practice of incarnation must locate itself within the context of *ecclesia* (Christian community) in order to be fully accountable to its historic New Testament mission. I develop this point more fully in chapter 4. It is honest to admit that it is often not easy to work out our spiritual identity in that context. But the church is the most resilient and grounded space with the dynamic ingredients of accountability, support, and the exercise of the gifts and fruits of the Spirit. The grammar of incarnational *agape* love is counter to the grammar of radical individualism, aloofness, cynicism, and agnosticism. The results are truly miraculous and transformative. Theology and *praxis* thereby become public automatically, challenging dehumanizing forces with transforming power and presence. The church practices this embodied, situated spirituality as a model of love and generosity, involving healthy sexual ethics as well as compassionate outreach and social justice. There remains more to follow on the profundity of *agape*, especially in chapter 5.

Epiphany is a key concept of encounter with the divine. It can also occur when painting or viewing a work of art. It speaks of a motivating, visible, divine presence and energy moving within culture, within the individual self. We are committed in this discourse to the engaging, incarnate truth. Called and commissioned disciples of Jesus rightfully expect, own, and share the miraculous, benevolent deeds together with the teachings of Jesus. They follow the intimations of Matt 25 in showing hospitality, caring for the stranger, the homeless refugee, and visiting the prisoner *in Jesus's name*. Messiah is articulated anew as suffering servant deeds, attitudes, and outlook. In the beginning, there was the Word and the Deed. Creation was Deed-Word: God spoke and there was light. Raymond Gawronski writes, "God's Word is so connected with God's deed that we can never distinguish between what is God's Word and what is God's deed in revelation."[36] They are intimately entwined, and so it must be with us as we face bravely our obligations and spiritual opportunities. Everything about Jesus was thoroughly word (teaching, insight) and everything about him was thoroughly deed (miracles, healing, compassion, inclusion). Seamlessly integrated, the deed explains the significance of the words, the teaching the significance of the deed or miracle. Jesus feeds the multitudes and then claims, "I am the Bread of Life" (John 6:35). He raises Lazarus from the dead and claims, "I am the Resurrection and the Life" (John 11:25). Christian community is grounded and nurtured in both the *word of God* and the *action of God*.

In summary, incarnational spiritual theology and praxis is rooted in profound underlying dynamics of unity: Creation and Redemption; Old and New Testaments (covenant-narratives); Christ and the Church. Once again, the New Testament makes the amazing claim that Jesus is, in the flesh, the wisdom of God and the power of God (1 Cor 1:24). I also recommend the sophisticated, scholarly understanding of incarnation in Wheaton College's New Testament scholar Daniel J. Treier.[37] Oliver O'Donovan puts the relationship between the divine and earthly realms in sharp focus. It begins with the uniqueness of God:

> Christ's particularity belongs to his divine nature, his universality to his human nature. As the one whom God has sent, he is irreplaceable; as the new man, he is the pattern to which we may conform ourselves.[38]

God's speech in Jesus is embodied, full-blooded, not flat, lifeless, or atomistic. Incarnation is a *communicative action*, much more than mere letters, words, or sentences. It is robust, loaded with spiritual vitality and meaning, heavily weighted with present and eternal consequences. It rings forth like an Oxford college bell—it is poetic, prophetic, and pedagogical. Incarnation as a dynamic *theodrama* means that *God has bound himself with humanity's very destiny*. We are stunned and at the same time transformed through contemplation of this truth. We urgently need to engage the veracity of incarnational spiritual culture—intellectually grasp it, feel it in our bones, live in solidarity with the miracle. This is a critical combination to avoid

---

36. Gawronski, *Word and Silence*, 166–69.

37. Treier, "Incarnation."

38. O'Donovan, *Resurrection and Moral Order*, 143–44.

Gnosticism on the road to unity, truth, beauty, and goodness, to fulsome, Christ-grounded wisdom and healthy religion.

PART III. FAITHFUL PRESENCE CAPTURES THE DYNAMIC WISDOM OF JESUS IN CULTURE

In the movie *Invictus*, South African president Nelson Mandela, played by actor Morgan Freeman, wisely displayed the following insight: Positive social change must begin with a different sense of identity, one where we become conscious of belonging to one another. He realized that individualism, divisiveness, tribalism, and radical self-interest was tearing his nation apart. They had to be redirected for corporate wellbeing, for the future survival of the nation. He chose to mobilize the forces of unity and the national rugby team was one key potential flashpoint. The ability of people of different races and interests to imagine their common destiny was key to breaking down racial barriers and healing decades-old resentments. Many of these resentments were exacerbated during the oppressive era of Apartheid. Things were at a boiling point.

The Springboks rugby team became a flashpoint for Mandela's quest for the common ground in his rainbow nation. He was able to get the whole nation and all races behind the team as they won the World Cup in 1995. At the time, there was only one black player, Chester Williams, but now there are several. Mandela showed intentional leadership wisdom as he offered a vision for a new inclusive humanism—speaking loudly, with humility and integrity, about solidarity with the marginalized. The book that tells the full story is *Playing the Enemy* by John Carlin.[39] Mandela won the world's admiration for his heroic efforts to reunite the country and redress terrible imbalances, racial tension, and injustice. He literally headed off a civil war. I have met one insider who relayed just how close things came to a major bloodbath during the election of Mandela in 1994. Many religious leaders—especially Anglican Bishop Desmond Tutu—and thousands of believers supported the vision and put much effort into its actualization. Significantly, Mandela forgave people who imprisoned him for twenty-six years and asked his fellow citizens to forgive wrongs done during the oppression of Apartheid (1948–94). Indeed, are we willing to *forgive* one another today amidst our culture wars? That is a very pressing issue.

39. Carlin, *Playing the Enemy.*

45

This argument for faithful presence builds on the previous section on incarnational wisdom. Incarnational spiritual culture likewise has such a vision for refocus, reinterpretation, re-presentation: reconfiguring relationships, wealth, and power in late modernity through peaceful means, with love at the core. This posture sets the stage for a new narrative of mutual flourishing, a new *social code* for life together.

> Thus, when the Word is enacted within the whole body of Christ in all of its members through an engagement that is individual, corporate, and institutional, not only does the word become flesh, but an entire lexicon and grammar becomes flesh in a living narrative that unfolds in the body of Christ; a narrative that points to God's redemptive purposes. It is authentic because it is enacted and finally persuasive because it reflects and reveals the *shalom* of God.[40]

Rooted in God's pursuit of us and his identification with us through sacrificial love, the incarnation is about *presence* rather than *absence*. Within its spiritual matrix, we want to explore further the dynamics of what renowned University of Virginia sociologist James Davison Hunter calls *faithful presence*.[41] Hunter's stance is very relevant to our late modern age. His project emphasizes witness and social change together with a mandate for servant leadership. It extends the concept of the suffering servanthood modeled by Jesus, leaving people with a trajectory to immediate relevance and cultural impact. Hunter highlights the urgency of this vision for our current cultural situation: filled with confusion, fragmentation, and cynicism. In the spirit of the incarnation, faithful presence offers a way to credibly rearticulate and reset the human narrative journey with a view to strengthening a person's identity. It allows humanity to find a new mandate: beyond the barbed wire of war, hate, chaos, resentment, cancel culture, and oppressive control. Hunter presses his point poignantly:

> Without a commitment to ideals that transcend the self and that direct life beyond self-interest, one is left with a despair that is not only joyless but also is indifferent towards need and thus incapable of addressing need. Hope is intimately tied to beauty for

40. Hunter, *To Change the World*, 254.

41. Hunter, *To Change the World*, 238–54. Hunter offers us a tremendous articulate grasp.

it is images of beauty and loveliness that inspire imagination and expand human possibility.[42]

This is true at a deep level. We use the language of *presence* to communicate this salient concept of closeness to the divine and God's closeness to us, but also in hospitality towards others. The vertical and horizontal dimensions coinhere. For example, the entire biblical narrative includes the offer of life marked by goodness, peace, truth, beauty, joy, and fruitfulness—*shalom*. Hunter writes that *shalom* also offers something rather significant to society at large as well. It would be quite astute for the Christian community to understand his trajectory. His inference is a robust sense of being with others and taking responsibility for the other, reminiscent of the project of French philosopher Emmanuel Lévinas. "The practice of faithful presence generates relationships and institutions that are fundamentally covenantal in character, the ends of which are the fostering of meaning, purpose, truth, beauty, belonging, and fairness—not just for Christians but for everyone."[43]

Notably, the *shalom* of God is the *presence* of God in the world (Eph 2:14). Incarnational community means that followers of Jesus are mandated to be and daily bring this *faithful presence*, this incarnational kind of humanism to their circles of influence, to daily work, to their neighborhood, to business and governance structures, and to family life. That is challenging indeed, requiring faith in Christ's assistance, listening to his voice for wisdom. We are called to pursue each other, identify with each other, and direct our lives towards the flourishing of one another. That sounds empowering, life-giving, and creative.

> A vision of order and harmony, fruitfulness and abundance, wholeness, beauty, joy and well-being. . . . Christians are to live toward the well-being of others, not just to those in the community of faith, but to all. . . . Pursuit, identification, the offer of life through sacrificial love—this is what God's faithful presence means. It is a quality of commitment that is active, not passive; intentional, not accidental; covenantal, not contractual. In the life of Christ we see how it entailed his complete attention. It was a whole-hearted, not half-hearted; focused and purposeful, nothing desultory about it. His very name, Immanuel, signifies all of this—"God with us"—in our presence.[44]

42. Hunter, *To Change the World*, 263.
43. Hunter, *To Change the World*, 263.
44. Hunter, *To Change the World*, 228, 230, and 243.

Faithful presence encourages us in our ascent towards the divine, while it develops outstanding character, as if we were climbing Mount Kilimanjaro. It offers a transformation of relationships within our open immanent frame, among the various culture spheres of science, ethics, religion, and aesthetics. It is also one that reaches beyond this frame for sources of the self, sources of the good. It is a powerful source of a *thick* identity that Charles Taylor speaks of in *Sources of the Self*,[45] one with resilience and sustainability. Servant leadership is a critical posture for this kind of engagement with the world. Such an engagement demands commitment from us and offers enduring promise.[46] People who carry this vision forward are now creating structures that incarnate blessing, manifest beauty, meaningfulness, and purpose for multitudes. They are not attempting to reinvent the world to suit their own self-interests, corruption, or internal self-contradictions. Incarnational community includes a diversity of former cynics, secularists, anarchists, and nihilists. It includes the privileged and the poor as well as people from other faiths. This incarnational posture stakes a claim on our life ambitions. Policy pursued and law legislated in light of the justice of God are indeed a witness to the right ordering of human affairs. Inquiry, scholarship, and learning with an awareness of the goodness of God's created order could be a catalyst for breakthrough. It could inspire some of our best research.

Moreover, Jesus offers this critical kind of wisdom in his life and teaching as Mark McMinn points out in *The Science of Virtue*.[47] Jesus challenged many of the religious systems of wisdom in place in his time. In the Sermon on the Mount, he challenges people's understanding of virtuous living. His wisdom is often countercultural, always discerning, sometimes mysterious, involving the odd social grenade. This displays critical thinking, with a high commitment to justice, mercy, goodness, and righteousness. Jesus shows incredible kindness and warmth to the disadvantaged and marginalized, even while he expresses outrage at the injustice of calcified religion and narcissistic leadership. He stands up to treachery, greed, and oppression. Among the marginalized that he advocated for in his time were: strangers, women and children, ethnic minorities, prodigals and sinners, widows and orphans, the poor, and the physically handicapped. He recognized the *imago Dei* in them, no matter how broken they appeared on first glance.

45. Taylor, *Sources of the Self*.
46. Brueggemann, *Gospel of Hope*.
47. McMinn, *Science of Virtue*.

Jesus, the perfect image of God, is the master of critical wisdom. He didn't come to abolish the traditional wisdom [of the Old Testament] but to enliven it, to flesh out the greatest commandments of loving God and loving neighbor as self, to remind us of life's deep mystery and to call us back to the fear and awe of God. We so easily settle for a religion composed of cognitive beliefs and behavioral lists that make us feel holier than others.[48]

PART IV. POWER THROUGH WEAKNESS: THE WISDOM AND SCANDAL OF THE CROSS

First Corinthians 1:18—2:16 shows Paul articulating the great power reversal: strength in weakness, wisdom in the foolish places, power in the weakest conditions. It is foolishness to the Greeks and a scandal for Jews. Christopher Watkin says it well:

> The cross is the gate through which all who wish to find God's power and wisdom must pass, a needle's eye. . . . Divine wisdom is not just the increase but the transfiguration of human wisdom; God's power is not the intensification but the transformative redemption of human power.[49]

According to Paul, the Christian cultural values of power and wisdom find their ultimate expression and fulfilment at the cross. Cultural stories only find their fulfillment, their completion in Jesus. He transforms, confronts, completes, and consoles the cultural narrative. This is why the Christian must engage and redeem culture, not just condemn it or write it off in disgust. Here lies true heroism. The cross is the center which fulfills all human desire. It turns our desires from selfishness to building a passion for God's will. These things are revealed by God's Spirit. Again Paul writes,

> Jews demand signs and Greeks look for wisdom, but we preach Christ crucified: a stumbling block to Jews and foolishness to Gentiles, but to those whom God has called, both Jews and Greeks, Christ the power of God and the wisdom of God. For the foolishness of God is wiser than human wisdom, and the weakness of God is stronger than human strength. (1 Cor 1:22–25)

---

48. McMinn, *Science of Virtue*, 26.
49. Watkin, *Biblical Critical Theory*, 429, 431.

This leads us into a short discussion of servant leadership. My doctoral mentor, John Webster of Christ Church, Oxford (now deceased) was a strong model of such leadership: a fine scholar and interlocutor. His support and patience was memorable and highly appreciated. He carried himself in a faithful, incarnational spiritual disposition.

PART V. SERVANT LEADERSHIP, THE PRACTICE OF WISDOM IN INCARNATIONAL CULTURE

On the platform of Christ's wisdom, we look for examples of incarnational spiritual *praxis*. One trajectory that emerges is the established and constructive culture of servant-leadership.[50] The basic principles of servant leadership are listening, empathy, healing, awareness, and persuasion. Other values are conceptualization, foresight, stewardship, building community, and commitment to the growth of people. Dr. Don Page is a former speechwriter for the Prime Minister of Canada, Pierre Trudeau, and Professor Emeritus at Trinity Western University where he developed and ran the Masters in Leadership Program. He has made a substantial contribution, in person and writing, to the incarnational spiritual culture which features servant-leadership. This includes work in China and Africa as well as North America through his inspiring *Servant-Empowered Leadership*.[51] Page casts a vision for the enduring productivity of servant-leadership to corporate, institutional, and church culture. It extends Hunter's idea of faithful presence within the spheres of the marketplace, government, healthcare, and education. He finesses the concept of skill set.

The gifts, resources, and influence that one stewards are not one's own to use as one wishes. Rather, according to Page, they belong to God. They exist under his authority, and believers are held to account for how they steward them for the common good. For example, it makes good sense that offering dignity and respect for employees creates a better work environment, and thereby a more successful company. It would be one where people are proud to work and give their best. Furthermore, using one's given resources for God's kingdom purposes creates significant opportunities and space for others to participate and develop their ideas. It stimulates creativity, co-operation, and collaboration among colleagues. It likewise champions the giftedness and potential of those we mentor and oversee. The focus is on

50. Greenleaf, *Power of Servant Leadership*; Page, *Servant-Empowered Leadership*.

51. Page, *Servant-Empowered Leadership*.

the physical, aesthetic, intellectual, spiritual, and social health of the work environment where we spend a remarkable amount of our time. Employees flourish under this approach, within this culture. The reason leadership is sacrificial and selfless is because its practice is an expression of *power under submission*. This is the opposite of Nietzsche's toxic concept of *will-to-power* dominance, which has fueled too much of corporate culture for too long.

Some striking examples of how such faithful presence works come to mind. It often starts with one person taking the incarnation vision seriously. This brave and wise person begins to live sacrificially and creatively for the benefit of others. One inspired person who wants to be faithful to the incarnational spiritual perspective of servant leadership is all it takes to begin a movement. Of course, it is even more powerful if the person is the head of a company or ministry, setting the whole *ethos* of the institution. Former Archbishop of Canterbury, Rowan Williams, writes about the Taizé Ecumenical Community in Burgundy, France. They have an enormous influence, capturing the imagination of many European youth who wanted to engage the world constructively. Taizé has ambassadorial cell groups living among the poor in Asia, Africa, and Latin America. This effort towards integral relationships amidst difference "represents a serious political concern, an eagerness to listen and learn across cultural boundaries, a sensitivity for certain styles in art and liturgy, traditional but spare and contemporary in expression, a profoundly contemplative spirituality."[52]

Dr. J. D. Hunter mentions a group in the state of Michigan, hit hard by the Financial Crisis of 2008. They took initiative and built not-for-profit housing to address the scourge of poverty and homelessness. A friend of mine mentioned a company that subsidized solar panels for poor areas and trained people in installing these for yet others. The Mennonite Central Committee sponsors *Ten Thousand Villages* stores with low overhead and many volunteers to assist talented artisans in developing nations to sell their work in the West, promoting their craft and giftedness globally. Students and faculty on campus at our university were captivated with the meaning of such a display in the student center. It displays and promotes faithful presence through creative, meaningful artisan work and loving distribution of their creative art. Art well-directed can speak of servant leadership. New York Times writer David Brooks features a strong vision for virtue and character development in his important contributions: *The Road to*

---

52. Williams, *Truce of God*, 124.

Character; and *The Second Mountain*.[53] These noble projects display excellent examples of personal risk and sacrifice, servant leadership, and faithful presence. They speak in *Word-Deed* language. They champion society as a whole, not just the elites or the exceptionally gifted. Below are Don Page's key servant-empowered leadership principles.

Principles of Servant-Empowered Leadership by Don Page (2009)

- Serves those we manage and leads for their benefit. Invests in people for their long-term growth.

- Primarily serves the interests of others above my selfish or narcissistic interests.

- Responsibility to those working with me is more important than my positional entitlements.

- Based on respect and love for others—maintained through internal influence, rooted in mutual trust.

- Willing to step aside for someone more qualified to lead. The position is held lightly. This can be a tough one to cultivate if one is quite invested over years of time.

- Never pulls rank to get one's own way, as that would be damaging to colleagues. This one has to be discerned situationally, because sometimes authority is important to solve a problem or hold someone accountable.

- Accountable to everyone in the organization and outside constituencies as well. Concerned about the common good, not just my individual good.

- Welcomes regular personal evaluations as a means of improving one's ability to serve. This kind of vulnerability speaks volumes, and the growth potential is palpable.

- Loyalty comes as a result of servant leadership's inspiration in the heart and soul of others. Servant leaders often have a low turnover rate because people feel valued (versus used) for their contribution to each other and to the organization.

---

53. Brooks, *Road to Character*; Brooks, *Second Mountain*.

- The primary interest is in the well-being of others, for their benefit. People on the team are seen as an end in themselves, not just a means to my ends.

- Puts the spotlight on others: Servant leaders are generous with praise for the accomplishments of others.

One vivid example of servant leadership comes via the feature film *The Way Out*. During World War II, four men manage to escape a Gulag Siberian labor camp in mid-winter. That was challenging enough, but they were then faced with the challenge of negotiating the Gobi Desert, and then climbing the Himalayas into India to freedom. This true story of superhuman endurance depicts dramatic, servant-empowered leadership. The wise leadership of the key player (a Polish man) makes all the difference in the perseverance and survival of the four. Often an individual is near exhaustion and expiration, but the leader keeps pulling them together as a group, cheering them onwards, caring for them individually.

In this chapter, we have discovered how Jesus offers foundational wisdom for the individual and human culture at large, not merely Christian culture. Incarnation impacts mankind as a whole. It respects human dignity, increases capacity, sets new precedents, and develops new vision for a better world. That is a bold claim, but there is good evidence that it works. Healthy, healing, life-supporting culture is always grounded in wisdom. In chapter 4, we explore our quest for a fuller, brighter experience of reality as it leads to redeemed relationality, receptivity, and agency within community and communion. This provides a new level of inquiry for our quest for incarnational spiritual culture. We continue in our quest towards the recovery of the *imago Dei*.

4

Incarnation
Individuals Engaged in Community

WE BEGIN THIS CHAPTER with some appropriate philosophical reflection together with Dr. Calvin Schrag in order to build on the previous discussion: "Community is constitutive of selfhood. It fleshes out the portrait of the self by engendering a shift of focus from the self as present to itself to the self as present *to, for* and *with* the other."[1] Many philosophers in late modernity lack a sense of the "we-experience" or the phenomenon of being-with-others. Michel Foucault, for example, is focused on freedom, aesthetics, and the art of self-care as a major goal, assuming individuals ought to produce an identity separate from community—something unique, even rebellious or revolutionary. Life for Foucault is about prying oneself loose from community obligations. This sentiment can easily be found in many other radically individualist late modern philosophers. The rhetoric of communal action, however, has an important role today: the idea of discovering and constituting oneself in fruitful relationship to others. This was one of the key themes to discern during my doctoral work. My own conclusions resonated with those of Professor Schrag. This is the same self that constitutes itself through discourse or narrative and embodied action.

> Community is more like a binding textuality of our discourse and
> the integrating purpose of our action. . . . Community, reminiscent
> of the ancient Greek concept of the polis, takes on a determination

1. Schrag, *Self after Postmodernity*, 78.

of value and is indicative of an ethico-moral dimension of human life. Self-understanding entails an understanding of oneself as a citizen of a polis, a player in an ongoing tradition of beliefs and commitments, a participant in an expanding range of institutions and traditions. Community is not a value-free description of a social state of affairs. The very notion of a communal being-with-others is linked to normativity and evaluative signifiers. . . . The discourse that is operative in the process of self-formation is a mixed discourse, in which the descriptive and the prescriptive, the denotative and evaluative, commingle and become entwined. . . . The "sociality" of being with is always already oriented either to-wards a creative and life-affirming intersubjectivity or towards a destructive and life-negating mode of being-with-others.[2]

The other major interlocutor with Foucault in my doctoral dissertation was eminent McGill University philosopher Charles Taylor. It is worthwhile to attempt to grasp his more communal orientation on identity in order to achieve an understanding of what it means to be a human subject. Taylor reveals the entwinement of personal identity with considerations of what constitutes the good life (ethics). He recognizes one's inherent interdependence with others. According to this take on reality, any philosophy of the self will also be a philosophy that embraces society and community. Thus, we need to recognize the historical and cultural features of self-constitution while attending to the ethico-moral fabric (*ethos*) of self-actualization. This involves both our *responsivity to* and our sense of *responsibility for* the other. *Ethos*, or what Taylor calls the *social imaginary* of a society, means a way of dwelling in a social world that gives rise to human goals and purposes, obligations, duties, and concerns for human rights. Well-respected British philosopher Roger Scruton agrees with this view of reality.[3]

As Taylor puts it, a "hermeneutics of understanding" take on reality means the self is never derived from itself alone. Rather, it finds itself within a language, a society, and a culture already in motion. Consequently, one's identity is already begun by virtue of one's responsibility to the speech or language game and actions of others. Parisian philosopher Emmanuel Lévinas also affirms this perspective,[4] showing that we realize our identity and responsibility in the *face of the other*. The Other constitutes a gift to us. But sometimes, there is terrible division, rivalry, conflict, and alienation,

2. Schrag, *Self after Postmodernity*, 86–88.
3. Scruton, *On Human Nature*.
4. Shepherd, *Gift of the Other*.

scapegoating, and even murder of the innocents. On our darker human side, we sadly often want others to suffer for us, we use them for our interests, or project our blame onto them. Corrupt dictators, in order to maintain power, make a whole country pay a high price through repression and oppression. They seek to atomize and divide people with fear and terror, even while they claim via propaganda that *they* are the great hope of the future, the uniting force for the country's common good.

PART I. THE DEBATE ON COMMUNAL IDENTITY: CHARLES TAYLOR DIALOGUES WITH MICHEL FOUCAULT

There are some critical questions to analyze at this juncture in our discussion of incarnational spiritual culture: How do we map our identity onto the communal landscape? Such a map is actually an articulation of one's *moral ontology*. Taylor claims that we are vitally linked to our moral framework.[5] How is identity formation interwoven with the constitution of the good life? How do we become a good or moral person? *Strong qualifications* or qualities of the will are vital to Taylor's notion of the moral self in the communal or intersubjective version of self-constitution or self-realization. The good is not a free-floating ideal, but truly something embedded in the human story and within community. This aspect of his moral ontology stands in stark contrast to Foucault's individualistic (*agonistic*) moral subjectivity.

In Taylor's view, the self is partly constituted by a language, one that necessarily exists and is maintained within a language community, among other selves who act as interlocutors.

> There is a sense in which one cannot be a self on one's own. I am a self only in relation to certain interlocutors: in one way in relation to those conversation partners who are essential to my achieving self-definition; in another in relation to those who are now crucial to my continuing grasp of language of self-understanding . . . a self exists only within . . . "webs of interlocution."[6]

These webs of interlocution prove significant for Taylor: the *Other* is seen as critical to one's moral self-constitution. In his view, there is a necessary, ongoing conversation with significant others which is critical to one's moral

5. Taylor, *Sources of the Self.*
6. Taylor, *Sources of the Self*, 36.

identity development. In Taylor's terms, there is a *myth* in Foucault's moral self, which says that one can define self in terms of a self-reflexive relationship with oneself alone, more explicitly, in relation to no communal web. Taylor contests that true creativity and originality demands that one should not work out their own unique identity solo.[7] From his perspective, this is not possible at a practical level. It is rather an abstract and unhealthy concept of what it means to be human—a self-manipulation. Thus, against the backdrop of Taylor's convictions about the play of the good in moral ontology, the character of Foucault's quest for freedom can lead in an unhealthy direction, towards the isolation of self or alienation, resulting in painful loneliness and resentment. This debate opens a key question of what elements are important to moral identity constitution and also what will support healthy agency and subjectivity. In the internet age, this is a crucial discussion.

These prominent *grande pensée* philosophers are locked in fundamental tension on this issue of self-definition with respect to community: Taylor's *communal* self contrasts starkly with the Foucault's radically *individualistic* self. Taylor contests this:

> I define who I am by defining where I speak from, in the family tree, in social space, in the geography of social statuses and functions, in my intimate relations to the ones I love, and also crucially in the space of moral and spiritual orientation within which my most important defining relations are lived out.[8]

In the first half of my dissertation, I outlined Foucault's ethics of freedom of expression and the modern-day *aesthetic* ideology of the self.[9] For Foucault, moral self-constitution means that one defines oneself over against the social matrix. Taylor disagrees and sees the benefits of a self which is integrated into a social matrix, even if withdrawing temporarily for perspective or personal healing. For example, a member of my family felt the need to leave home as a young teen in a kind of *Foucauldian rebellion*. Later on with maturity and some tough, real-world experience, he comes to realize the importance of family as a space to nurture his identity. This was an *epiphany* for the prodigal son who came home to reassess the meaning of life, in a more Taylorian fashion.

7. Taylor, *Sources of the Self*, 39.
8. Taylor, *Sources of the Self*, 35.
9. Eagleton, *Ideology of the Aesthetic*.

Foucault sees the need for disruption, while Taylor pursues integration—two radically different stances. Taylor notes that even from one's earliest years, one's moral language must inevitably be tested on others (*triangulation*). University of Virginia educator and author Matthew Crawford agrees, contending that the lack of such dialogue can lead to a kind of tragic and vulnerable *moral autism*.[10] This is a serious handicap for many Millennials and Generation Z. Gradually, says Taylor, through this sort of relational-moral-conversation, the individual gains confidence in what it means and in *who* they are as a moral and spiritual being—a citizen. This is no small thing. It is quite a profound aspect of what it means to be human, to grasp one's *metabiological* meaning. Others must be granted intrinsic value, a voice, and presence for this dialogue to be effective and life-affirming. The key is to find some wise and responsible interlocutors and mentors, both within one's greater family and beyond. Those who neglect this task often feel lost and disoriented. They lack important direction and validation. Family members who are alienated from one another experience great existential pain.

One is transformed by the lives, the wisdom, and deeper understanding of significant others. Our elders and mentors are vitally important to our own emergence as critical thinkers and choosing agents. Taking this discussion a step further, Taylor argues for a self that is socially embedded in its moral constitution. One relates to the moral good, not only as an individual self, but within a communal context, where the community also incarnates some good or goods, some ideals, principles, or standards of appropriate behavior. Some would use the language of values, virtues, and moral convictions. This stands in stark contrast to the distinct lack of *we* language in Foucault's grammar of the moral self. He instead promotes a more decontextualized, aesthetic, self-reflexive self—one which embraces *agonisme* with respect to the social sphere. He is especially skeptical of social constructions of the good which we find in religious groups, even though this is exactly what he is doing: he is making a social construction of self as a radical individualist. The individualized self becomes his religion. The communal and narrative dimensions of self are not on Foucault's hermeneutical map; his is a hermeneutic of suspicion. He makes a move during his third *oeuvre* in his thinking to recover agency—after his Power-Knowledge stage. But he lacks a full, robust version of healthy subjectivity. Here's an insightful quote from critic William Connolly:

10. Crawford, *World Beyond Your Head*, 183–85.

Foucault . . . cannot endorse this quest for attunement and self-realization. He proceeds at the second level, as a genealogist, deploying rhetorical devices to incite the experience of discord or discrepancy between the social construction of self, truth, and rationality and that which does not fit neatly. And the recurrent experience of discord eventually shakes the self loose from the quest for a world of harmonization, a world in which institutional possibilities for personal identity harmonize with a unified set of potentialities in the self, and the realization of unity in the self harmonizes with the common good realized in the social order. This quest for identity through institutional identification becomes redefined as the dangerous extension of "disciplinary society" into new corners of modern life. Genealogy exercises a claim upon the self that unsettles the urge to give hegemony to the will to truth.[11]

Community or communal identity, however, for Taylor does not entail uniformity, or a dull conformity or unthinking conventionalism. He is more optimistic about a dynamic, transformative, renewing, growing economy of *being-with-others*. Community can thrive even when there is disagreement between interlocutors. He opens up this theme beautifully and profoundly in *The Language Animal*.[12] But one cannot have community without some sort of normativity, some common commitment to the moral good and to an objective *higher good*. The loss of normativity often brings on anxiety and identity crisis. He is strong on the position that there is no such thing as a value-neutral, intersubjective state of affairs. It should come as no surprise that there is a strong link between Foucault's avoidance of community and his transgressive attitude towards normative ethics. We also see that in society today with radical individualists and anti-social players of various sorts.

Genuine, authentic community cannot exist without the normative—there must be a good or goods, virtues, or values that we hold in common to create social bonding and communal sanity. This element is essential to trust and mutual respect, to the smooth functioning of society such as in democracy and social justice. The interpretation of self in terms of its relation to the good can only proceed in recognition of self's interdependence with other selves. We must be mutually concerned about the interests of others as well as our own, realizing the ways in which we have common cause and mutual contextual needs. Taylor presses Foucault here: "The

11. Connolly, *Michel Foucault: An Exchange*, 365.

12. Taylor, *Language Animal*, chs. 6–8.

drive to original vision will be hampered, will ultimately be lost in inner confusion, unless it can be placed in some way in relation to the language and vision of others."[13] Taylor's vision is clearly more compatible with the wisdom and vision of incarnational spiritual culture.

Foucault's *thin* version of self is intentionally abstracted out of community—in order to maximize pleasure—and out of narrative continuity. This is said to be because of a concern to avoid domination and manipulation by the other, added to a need to resist or manipulate power relations to one's own advantage. But is he not also advocating a diminishment of self? This seems like a classic overreach of the *power relations* and *truth games* rhetoric. The following is a striking application of my meaning: Matthew Crawford has some brilliant insights in his insightful *The World Beyond Your Head.*[14] He suggests that our quest for radical individualism and autonomy is leading us into an unhealthy *moral autism.* Corporately in the West, we are progressively losing our moral skill, power, and agency. Crawford calls this the cult of sincerity, a version of overdetermined subjectivism: "It leaves people bereft of any public language in which to express their intuitions about the better or worse, the noble or shameful, the beautiful and ugly, and *assert them as valid.*"[15] It offers far too much sovereignty to the individual's feelings (aesthetic ethics) and not enough to mutual accountability. He says that we actually need others, such as friends, family, and colleagues, to check our own self-understanding—through a process called *triangulation.* They let us know when we are doing well, that we are good, excellent, or not so good. We also refer to it as *validation.* One trait that distinguishes us universally as humans is our continual desire to justify ourselves and our behavior. Guilt, self-dislike, and shame result if we are unable to do so. It is a fundamental truth that we never act without moral implications and connotations. When all this is said, we need a web of people to act as a sociality of normativity. Taylor strongly agrees.[16]

Now here is the real gravity of our late modern cultural situation. In times of cultural flux, where it is unclear what the rules are, it is quite difficult for us to understand ourselves, nor how to value things or identify noble behavior. This leads to what psychologists and psychotherapists are calling an ongoing *existential identity crisis.* As a direct consequence, we

13. Taylor, *Sources of the Self,* 37.

14. Crawford, *World Beyond Your Head.*

15. Crawford, *World Beyond Your Head,* 184.

16. Taylor, *Sources of the Self.*

become victims of the values of the transactional marketplace—productivity, performance, usefulness, cash-out value. Psychologist Alain Ehrenberg notes that this is leading to epidemic levels of workaholism and depression in our culture of high performance.[17] Enough is never enough for our employers and the bottom line: "Depression presents itself as an illness of responsibility in which the dominant feeling is one of failure. The depressed individual is unable to measure up; he is tired of having to become himself."[18] Consequently, in a culture of performance, "the person reads the value and status of her soul in terms of her worldly accomplishments."[19] She remains guilt-ridden and stressed, always faced with the raw issue of raising the bar: like increasing those billable hours. This puts constant pressure on the employee's capacity, leading to pathological weariness, headaches and poor relationships. When do I have time to meet someone or go on a date when I am working ninety hours a week? We clearly need other values, virtues, or moral goods, in order to round out our identity, to prevent workaholism and catastrophic burnout.

In addition, it is difficult to mitigate this depression in our age of performance and commodification, because in a catch-22, weariness comes to equal weakness in the eyes of our supervisors and peers. So we turn to quick fixes, stimulants like Prozac or Adderall (an amphetamine), and even cocaine to maintain our *high-performance* lifestyle. There appears to be an epidemic use of these drugs among students and young faculty in high-performance universities, or traders on Wall Street. Students that I am in dialogue with strongly affirm. While we seek liberation through this autonomy, we are falling victim to a very toxic slavery to self-productivity. Modernity and its idealized individualism has turned on us. Paul the apostle, in the book of Ephesians, believes that growing our identity in Christ can give us perspective and reprieve from such pressure. We will cover more on this later in the book.

In fact, we need both freedom and accountability for balanced mental health. Libertarians emphasize freedom but give us no account of its origins, or its contextuality. Communitarians emphasize accountability to the social body, but do not emphasize enough the importance of individuality and personal choice. They both display only half of the truth. Freedom and accountability are in fact coextensive in the human agent; they are linked

17. Ehrenberg, *Weariness of the Self*.
18. Ehrenberg, *Weariness of the Self*, 4.
19. Crawford, *World Beyond Your Head*, 162.

by their very nature. The truly free person is always taking account of others in order to coordinate her presence and actions with theirs. This person is happy to give constructive reasons for their behavior that carry weight with the other and contribute to the good of the whole, with a view to harmony. We exist in a social context and that is where true freedom plays the game well. Virtue practice like wisdom, humility, gratitude, and love show us how to play the game of life wisely. Humans find their true fulfillment in mutual love and self-giving.

PART II. THE EMBODIED AND COMMUNAL NATURE OF INCARNATIONAL SPIRITUAL CULTURE

We are deeply affected by our loves, our longings, and desires. Our hopes and dreams are key to our identity. Creative life within the right community can build an upward and expansive momentum for young adults. Incarnational spirituality frees us to renounce dysfunctional *expressive individualism*, replacing it with humble servant leadership, mutual affection and hospitality. The objective we speak of moves us towards a virtue-oriented society of co-flourishers, marked by cooperation and collaboration. Competition will, of course, always remain to some degree, but this spiritual identity moves us away from radical self-interest toward appreciation and a sense of responsibility for others. In Kierkegaard's terminology, we move from the *aesthetic* level of identity to the *ethical*. We escape our aloofness, self-indulgence, and indifference, the neuroses of the proud, aesthetic self. We enter courageously into embedded, embodied vulnerability in the covenantal trust of *I-Thou* relationality. It leads us out of our sensuality and narcissism into grounded and dynamic group adventure.

Here Calvin Schrag draws on Merleau-Ponty's phenomenology of embodiment:

> His seminal description and analysis of the structure and dynamics of what he came to call "the lived body," which he distinguished from the human body as an object of physiological mechanics that derived its categorical matrix and principles of explanation from investigation of physical substance in general. The body as lived is veritably who I am. The body as concrete embodiment is the site of tasks to be performed and projects to be carried through. The who of action, comprehending the world in and through his or her

action, is an embodied subject with idiosyncratic features of lived spatiality and lived mobility.[20]

Thus, my body is in effect my center of vision, action, and interest—it is I myself. I am not a *ghost in a machine* like the *cogito* in René Descartes. Rather, it is a matter of incarnate consciousness of the self as embodied personhood. Comprehension of incarnation begins with the individual, then God in human flesh, then Christ indwelling his church, his body (Eph 4) by means of the Holy Spirit. It is a trinitarian communality and communion (chapter 5). We can say, as we might in our wedding vows, "This is my body, this is all of me given to you for your nourishment and spiritual growth." Such is the incarnational trajectory of a life biography.

In Part III of *The Physical Nature of Christianity*, Warren Brown and Brad Strawn write about *complex dynamical systems* and how this relates to Christian spiritual formation.[21] Their claim is that these complex, dynamical systems are *the* key context in which people change and are transformed. It is often assumed that speaking to the individual, teaching the Bible and encouraging them to change for the better or to set high goals is the key strategic component of discipleship. However, while the individual remains important, it is our significant relationships that actually heal us and shape us most profoundly. Many counselors and psychologists would corroborate this claim. Think of how important the social recovery support structure is of *the meeting*. We see this individual-communal tension playing out among the high achiever surgeons on the television show *Grey's Anatomy*. Without reconciling significant relationships at home or work, they are held back from performing surgery and patient care optimally.

Brown and Strawn strongly emphasize the importance of paying more attention to entities like social networks: mutual shaping experiences, small groups, clusters of relationships, and mutual imitative reinforcement. They appropriately draw these ideas from research in the social and behavioral sciences. This is precisely why immersive group retreats or conferences are remembered for much longer than a good sermon or lecture. Significant conversations during such events can be quite transformative. This is also why good collegiality can inspire and empower us through problem solving and exchange of ideas. I still remember my first large Christian conference as an undergraduate called Urbana with 15,000 university students and some of the best mission-minded speakers and teachers in the world. The

20. Schrag, *Self after Postmodernity*, 48, 54.

21. Brown and Strawn, *Physical Nature of Christianity*, 101–57.

sincerity and zeal of the participants rocked my world and impacted my future vocation. The research by Brown and Strawn offers vital advice for leaders and educators, both religious and secular. Sometimes, in the case of church ministry, we often focus too intensely on the individual disciple or potential believer. We feed them the good theological information, with hopes of building their character or setting their destiny. But are we not catering to the dangerous ideal of radical individualism and the *aesthetic or consumer self*, where we are too oriented to pitching things to the desires of individual entitlement. Quite often, we tragically miss the importance of communal identity. I have witnessed this mysterious dynamic in student ministry on several occasions.

Social formation of people within networks and clusters begs for more attention as we seek to model ourselves after the personal dynamics of the Trinity, and on Christ as definitive *imago Dei*. Incarnation is definitely not a conspiracy theory; there is nothing secret or coded about it. It is public, accessible, clear knowledge. Christopher Watkin captures the thrust succinctly:

> The ultimate truth and reality of the universe steps into the universe in a way that confounds the rationalists and the conspiracy theorists alike. Ultimate reality is manifest in the grubbiness of the everyday, in Christ's sinewy flesh, at a particular moment in history rather than on a "meta" level of abstract explanation separate from those particular, historical events.[22]

Generation Z will be well-served by leaders and teaches sensitive to this grass roots, communal approach. They will be mobilized to contribute through these powerful small groups and networks, support groups for retrieval of the good and robust identity formation. In communal contexts, they can begin to learn the art and genius of care, self-giving, and *agape* love. Ghosts can be transformed into givers, value-adding entrepreneurs, and lively covenant participants as they come to grips with the grace and truth that a relationship with Jesus delivers within loving community. As mutual trust and commitment grows, it is much easier to ask for help to heal from one's loneliness, addictions, or woundedness, one's sense of inadequacy or lack of direction. Social networks offer a positive environment for wounded healers. I can strongly attest to the value of this approach during my formative undergraduate years in the Life Sciences at Queen's University. My network in different institutions and with friends was a lifeline: a source of moral,

22. Watkin, *Biblical Critical Theory*, 369.

intellectual, and theological growth. Many of those friendships have lasted a lifetime and continue to inspire and challenge me.

The notion of giving oneself in love characterizes Balthasar's view of reality—from the relations within the Trinity through to the creation, incarnation and the saving work of Christ.[23] The unfathomable goodness and love of God meets humanity through the incarnation, on understandable and practical terms. Jesus Christ addresses each human individually. At the same time, he draws them into a family environment leading to a richer, *thick* identity. They see and are seen, know and are known, accept and are accepted, experience hospitality and generously share their resources with others. This process of maturity comes to full fruition within dynamic community and creative dialogue, producing growing communion. Furthermore, the process bestows a substantial dignity and healthy self-worth that makes one more human, more personal, more at home with self in a hostile world. We are not fully ourselves until integrated into community with other humans beings and God, until we actualize this incarnational spiritual culture in our own personal life.

The *A Rocha Community* in White Rock, British Columbia, Canada is a lively example of such dynamic networks. Their core values are Christian spirituality, conservation, community, and cooperation across cultures. Each center incarnates the practice of *shalom* and faithful presence. These teaching-living-working units exist in twenty-two countries. The organization was started by Peter and Miranda Harris.[24]

> Jesus brings us home, Jesus brings us together, Jesus breaks down hostility, Jesus creates us as a unified humanity, Jesus reconciles all of us to God. Peace is complex and many-layered. A lot of action goes into making peace and Jesus *is* the action. . . . Church is where peace is understood comprehensively as Christ present and working among us.[25]

---

23. Gawronski, *Word and Silence*, 163.

24. See https://arocha.ca.

25. Peterson, *Practice Resurrection*, 124, 126.

PART III. INCARNATIONAL CULTURE FEATURES NARRATIVE SELVES

Furthermore, incarnational culture reminds us that we are *storied*, communal selves within a committed covenant, as opposed to ghostly techno-hermits playing video games endlessly. Respected American sociologist, Brené Brown, in *Rising Strong*[26] urges that we need to own our stories however joyful, difficult, or pain-filled. Most experts will agree. Stories are of high value, irreplaceable, necessary to our identity. Brown also offers hope that we can *rewrite* them with different outcomes, thereby transcending fate, despair, addiction, dysfunctionality, and shame. But we dare not attempt to accomplish this alone. Without community and a larger story of grace, redemption, and recovery, we would never begin to envision or actualize personally such transformational promise. The Bible contains such a true-to-life large narrative with a fascinating variety of characters seeking their destiny and fortune while wrestling with their demons. Seekers can access this narrative at several junctures as a means to enter the reflective, meaningful life. Christopher Watkin is a phenomenally gifted expert on the biblical narrative as a platform from which to view culture critically.[27] Walter C. Kaiser Jr.[28] inspired me as a graduate student about the powerful promise theme that runs like a mighty river through Scripture.

Hermeneutically within the incarnation narrative, Christ's whole story of teaching, sacrificial death, resurrection, and ascension turn out to be the core inner logic of Scripture, the story of stories, the fulfillment of the great promise theme. As I have already demonstrated, the biblical narrative reveals human failure to live faithfully the *imago Dei*, but it redemptively shows us how to regain access to God's grace and healing. Biblical theologians like Richard Middleton show us that the drama of the Word unfolds profoundly in the breadth of Scripture from Genesis to Revelation.[29] He also adeptly traces the emergence of the meaning of the *imago Dei* throughout the entire biblical narrative, work that he accomplished in his doctoral dissertation. I met Middleton as a very curious graduate student in philosophy at University of Guelph.

26. Brown, *Rising Strong*, 39–43.

27. Watkin, *Biblical Critical Theory*.

28. Kaiser, *Promise Plan of God*.

29. Middleton, *Liberating Image*.

People tend to see the world through the lens of their beliefs, including unconscious ones. This is how they seek purpose and meaning in life, make sense of their experience. This is how they begin to script their narrative. We all need an existential (*meta-biological*) reason for why we exist, for our purpose in life, beyond the arc of biological survival. We are so much more than our DNA, neuronal networks, and animal bodies. These worldview beliefs vary widely, impacting current cultural debates. They range from religious or spiritual convictions to agnosticism, pure atheism or nihilism. Nihilism is a deeply cynical view that ironically proposes *the meaning of meaninglessness*. Duke professor of philosophy Alex Rosenberg is an example of a consistent nihilist. He argues that if we start with assumptions of naturalism or atheism, there is no basis for human rights, worth, or dignity of the individual—that is, if we are consistent with a materialistic philosophical worldview. Notre Dame sociologist Christian Smith writes profoundly about the overreach of many atheistic worldviews, but agrees that Rosenberg is coherent.[30] Smith wonders how indeed we can sustain universal benevolence and human rights if we in the West lose or discard our Judeo-Christian heritage. This is the million-dollar question: What will give us warrant and motivation regarding the good and the common good, virtues and value of communal wellbeing, individual rights and human worth?

In his articulation of moral mapping, eminent Canadian philosopher Charles Taylor looks to narrative depth as a defining feature of the spiritual self, identity, and agency. Narrative is consequential to the stability and continuity of the moral self over time. It comes in the shape of a personal *quest*, the notion of self as a narrative quest. He gets this from Catholic ethical philosopher Alasdair MacIntyre.[31] Narration of the quest for the good allows one to discover a unity amidst the diversity of goods or noble ideals that demand one's attention. It is especially true of his category *hypergood*—which helps coordinate and prioritize the various goods in one's moral horizon. We have spoken of *agape* love as exemplary of such a *hypergood*. The healthy continuity of the self through life is a necessary part of a life lived robustly: with integrity, resilience, and weight. Along with Paul Ricoeur, he sees narrative as a key component of the deep structure of self, a temporal depth in his *thick* concept of the self (historical-moral-spiritual-identity).

30. Smith, *Atheist Overreach*, ch. 2, "Does Naturalism Warrant Belief in Universal Benevolence and Human Rights?," pp. 45–86.

31. Taylor, *Sources of the Self*, 17, 48.

This reveals another rich, interwoven strand in the communal view of identity.

The good is more than a concept outside the self, an ideal of a life lived well. It is also something embodied, carried in one's story and the story of one's community. For example, Mennonites are well-known for their hospitality, concern for refugees, and practical care. Community narrative is a powerful way to mediate the good to a younger generation. Our lives are empowered by the good; our passions and motivations are fueled by the good. Taylor writes,

> This sense of the good has to be woven into my understanding of my life as an unfolding story. . . . Making sense of my life as a story is not an optional extra. . . . There is a space of questions which only a coherent narrative can answer.[32]

In this sense, my story is what makes sense of me and my network or group of interlocutors. We could well explore the kind of questions a healthy narrative can answer. The key issue is the unity and past-present-future continuity of life. This is to be contrasted with a strong focus of the self-as-discontinuity (the prodigal self)—where the quest is to *get free of oneself*, of one's past upbringing or tradition. For example, the movement for Foucault is towards the ever-new, reinvented self, a self which dislikes vulnerability, and tries to avoid being known by the Other, wedging itself loose from history, institutions, and community—the dis-integrated self. Taylor's narrative depth is not at all a priority for Foucault, and there is a minimum interest in continuity of life with the past. This causes serious narrative brokenness. Foucault promotes a very future-oriented, consumeristic, pleasure-seeking, aesthetic self with beauty as a top priority. It is one that wants to escape the oppression of one's past, power-knowledge, and normalization. His quest is for uniqueness and originality. We see this philosophical bent working itself out in our current cultural Marxism, a revolution in thought within the humanities and gender studies.[33] A social moral norm and metanarrative reads as a prison for Foucault and for many of a younger generation.

Taylor protests: He believes that one's story, properly understood, is an essential part of what constitutes the moral self—one's identity. For him, it becomes relevant to ask, "What has shaped me thus far?" and again, "What

32. Taylor, *Sources of the Self,* 47.

33. Trueman, *Rise and Triumph.* He offers a robust history of this movement and the power of the aesthetic culture sphere.

direction is my life taking in terms of the good?" or "Does my life have weight and substance?"[34] Taylor suggests that a healthy self must explore questions about the larger span of life, beyond the here and now. The resilient person is not only interested in the immediate present, or an escape into a fantastic future. He writes, "My sense of the good has to be woven into my life as an unfolding story."[35]

The pressing question in this dialogue between Taylor and Foucault is this: What is the direction to substantial, mature freedom and a sound future? Is it the calculated deconstruction of the burdensome past? Alternatively, is it fathoming one's narrative depth of identity and marking out the trajectory of one's narrative quest, in order to make sense of one's story and grow into it as a calling? Taylor wants to argue for *executive control* over one's story, mitigating the pressures of cultural trendiness or mediocre conformity (playing the game). Tied into this quest is the concept of a *call* on one's life; for him, a sense of call is crucial to one's narrative trajectory. Indeed, it is possible to map out the future with a set of short-term and long-term goals, and yet have no resounding depth to it—producing a trivial self, a far less meaningful life. Within the biblical narrative, nothing of our experience seems wasted. Even our mistakes, sins, and failures can be redeemed for our education and future good. We can be freed to grow up into a healthy accountability and responsibility stance. British philosopher Roger Scrutin chimes in at this juncture to add insight on the depth of personhood. Virtues are dispositions that we praise and their absence is a matter of shame:

> Virtue consists in the ability to take full responsibility for one's acts, intentions, and avowals, in the face of all the motives for renouncing or denouncing them. It is the ability to retain and sustain the first-person center of one's life and emotions, in face of the decentering temptations with which we are surrounded and which reflect the fact that we are human beings, with animal fears and appetites, and not transcendental subjects, motivated by reason alone.[36]

My narrative is my weight, my substance. In his more recent tome, *The Language Animal*, Charles Taylor writes, "Stories give us an understanding of life, people, and what happens to them which is peculiar (distinct from

34. Taylor, *Sources of the Self*, 50.
35. Taylor, *Sources of the Self*, 47.
36. Scruton, *On Human Nature*, 100.

what other forms, like works of science and philosophy), and this is also [without substitute]."[37] A key insight here is that "It is through story that we find or devise ways of living bearably in time."[38] Good stories can offer us transcendence over change, over challenging and tedious circumstances. This sense of continuity reduces our level of anxiety about the future. We must have a *take* on reality or we entertain an identity crisis or at least a very boring, minimalist existence. The way that I tell my story shapes my identity, it is central to being a healthy individual. It may be intriguing to discover that we each have an inner biographer—linking past, present, and future mental states and experiences. This kind of temporal (*diachronic*) mapping is critical to a healthy identity: Where have I come from? Where am I going? What time is it now in my story? What are my challenges and opportunities? What are my goals and contributions to family and culture?[39] Truly, it is imperative that I care about my future self, at least as much as my present self. Narrative is a vital ticket to my overall social, psychological, and spiritual wellbeing. Indeed, we also need great stories to make sense of society as a whole.

In this argument for the narrative dimensions of the self, Taylor draws on the great French philosopher Paul Ricoeur who has written extensively on the important difference between *ipse* and *idem* identity.[40] Idem identity refers to the objective stability of one's identity over time (read as a succession of moments) and outside time (character traits that don't change with time). *Ipse identity* is more fluid and dynamic, as per one's personal identity as an unfolding character in a novel. It develops in the temporal *becoming* of the self, its moral and spiritual growth over time. The concept is absolutely fascinating. *Ipse identity* is carried through memory and anticipation, and linked with narrative temporality. Crucial to *ipse-identity* is the ongoing integration of past, present, and future in a unified fashion, a narrative unity.[41] This should help us understand why people like our parents in their seventies want to review their whole story. Many a story relates the journey from childhood to adulthood, one of moral growth (*bildungsroman*). This often makes the basis of a good movie or play. It is why Alzheimer's disease

---

37. Taylor, *Language Animal*, 291.

38. Taylor, *Language Animal*, 319.

39. Wolterstorff, *In This World of Wonders*. A great philosopher invites us into his story.

40. Ricoeur, *Oneself as Another*, 113–68.

41. Taylor, *Sources of the Self*, 50.

is such a tragedy for families, where a senior loses track of the storyline of their life, sometimes forgetting the identity of those closest to them. We clearly can take this quest for a working narrative much more seriously.

There are two significant implications of these two features of identity through time. One is the possibility of the future as different from the present and past, the possibility of redeeming the past, in order to make it a part of the meaning of one's life story.[42] It is to bring a fresh interpretation, for instance, on one's suffering, failures, and disappointments. Foucault wants this kind of transcendence: a new future for the self, one which is self-created. But narrative does not allow for a discontinuity with the past, a refusal of past identity or origins. Taylor cautions,

> To repudiate my childhood as unredeemable in this sense is to accept a kind of mutilation as a person; it is to fail to meet the full challenge involved in making sense of my life. This is the sense in which it is not up for arbitrary determination what the temporal limits of my personhood are.[43]

You may have watched the Jason Bourne series of movies where a trained CIA black ops assassin is desperate to recall and recover his memory, and his story. He is experiencing an existential crisis and it will not let him rest. The past, grappling with the meaning of the past, seeking healing from past hurts, trauma, and failures is vital to his healthy narrative self. Taylor agrees with Foucault that it makes sense to set a future trajectory for one's life, to project a future story. This promotes the sense that one's life has a direction and purpose.[44] He is equally open to personal creativity.

> Because we cannot but orient ourselves to the good, and thus determine our place relative to it and hence the direction of our lives, we must inescapably understand our lives in narrative form, as a "quest."[45]

This quest requires a *telos* or goal, and for this, a robust knowledge of the good (our ideals) is required. Taylor believes in narrative in the *strong* sense—a structure inherent in human experience and action, narrative as a human *given*. It is an essential part of one's reflective life and self-interpretation. Identity *in Christ* takes seriously our past while helping

42. Taylor, *Sources of the Self*, 51.
43. Taylor, *Sources of the Self*, 51.
44. Taylor, *Sources of the Self*, 48.
45. Taylor, *Sources of the Self*, 51–52.

us to chart a promising future. We don't have to get stuck in the past with its hurts, dysfunctionality, and resentments. The Jesus story itself exemplifies his making sense of his Messianic identity and the larger meaning of the incarnation. During all this time, he is deeply aware of his relationship with the Father and the Holy Spirit. He knows his calling and he follows through with it consistently and courageously. Journalist David Brooks writes eloquently about this moral growth purpose from his personal story in *The Second Mountain*.[46] This narrative in turn is embedded in community where one is accountable, where one learns from other narratives and other storytellers. We often ask ourselves, "What are my university friends and roommates now doing with their lives? Are they following a strong and secure calling or quest, or are they traveling in circles?"

For Foucault, and for many today, the trajectory of the quest is definitely towards the beautiful (aesthetic feelings, the beautiful life, self as a work of art) which includes freedom from responsibility, rather than freedom to pursue the good or the common good. There is a distinct and tragic loss of moral reference points and parameters in this age of cultural revolution in late modernity. See especially on this point the fine work by Carl R. Trueman.[47] Many have failed to make the mature move from the *aesthetic* to the *ethical* and on to the *religious* (Kierkegaard). From Taylor's perspective, Foucault is suggesting a self-articulation that attempts an escape from one's earlier, historical self, excising oneself from past identity. The assumption here is that the earlier self is locked in the iron cage of institutional *power/knowledge*. This is seen to prevent the future self from a positive emergence into full freedom and creative flourishing. Foucault's focus of concern is the *becoming* self (*ipse* identity), the *re-scripting or reconstruction* of self. But he is very weak on the *idem identity*. There is a major difference between Foucault and Taylor on the stability of the future self. This is a concern carried by adopted children, since there is a radical break with their origins. They will ask over and over, "Why did my birth mother and father abandon me? Did they not love me? Am I worthless?"

Taylor's approach maintains continuity with the past, attempting to resolve past issues, disappointments, trauma, and pain. Foucault maintains a radical discontinuity with the past, seeing a need to deconstruct it, escape it, disrupt its hold on him. The assumption is that one must change one's identity in order to hide from the chains and the pain of the past (the

46. Brooks, *Second Mountain*.

47. Trueman, *Rise and Triumph*.

fugitive stance). There is a difficulty here. The pursuit of a complete, discontinuous reinvention of self, which Foucault celebrates, is to court psychosis and possibly to do oneself personal damage.[48] It is easy to imagine that some very extreme forms of life could emerge out of assuming such discontinuity and experimentation. Imagine a lying, murderous, narcissistic dictator or criminal who refuses accountability for his past actions. In Taylor, on the other hand, the good is interlaced with narrative and community in order to provide the self with infrastructure, roots, accountability, and depth of meaning. The quest should be to resolve the issues and problems of the past in order to maintain one's integrity and to heal from past hurts. This is also entailed within the deeper trajectory of incarnational spiritual culture.

One very rewarding personal example of this trajectory of self is our ongoing connection with alumni from our ministry on various university campuses in Ontario and British Columbia, Canada, and the United Kingdom. They remind us of the great dialogue we had when they were being formed as undergrads and postgraduate students. It is great to see them shine in their careers and lives and to savor the memories of adventures and discoveries at University of British Columbia, Waterloo, Wilfrid Laurier, Guelph, Queen's, and Oxford. The other historical memory is the great books in my library and the weighty history of the stimulating lectures we have both attended and sponsored over a number of decades. Another great sense of history and powerful, life-giving story was my engagement with the excellent Oxford University libraries and my mentor theologian John Webster from Christ Church and Second Reader philosopher Donn Welton from Stony Brook University during my doctoral studies. There is much to celebrate and savor in each of our stories. Good stories energize us for future contributions and fruitful impact.

PART IV. BIBLICAL INCARNATE SPIRITUAL COMMUNITY: THE WAY TO RE-ENCHANTMENT

With the previous discussion on community and narrative depth in mind, we can now read the Old Testament (Hebrew Bible) with fresh eyes, employing the Jesus story—an active *Christological reading*. In light of Christ, we can capture the full narrative journey *away from God, back to God, with God, for God, to the glory of God* (lostness, alienation, recovery, reckoning, communion). It is powerful to see the entire biblical narrative as the

48. Taylor, *Sources of the Self*, 51.

vehicle for God's transformative work in human culture.[49] God pursues us consistently as Abraham Heschel has articulated so well, he works with us even at our most dysfunctional. Jesus's life reveals that God loves prodigals, meaning that our story can turn around. We don't have to settle for magic or fate to precariously navigate life. Redemption through the incarnate Christ blossoms into harmonious social communion, while maintaining a strong respect for individuality. "In redeeming the created order, Christ redeems social relationships among creatures, relationships that are intrinsic to created human nature."[50] This is the river that runs through our quest for re-enchantment, our search for our true home.

It is the incarnate, suffering, dying, rising man Jesus of Nazareth who at the core of his being shows the way to intimacy with God, gives glory to God in everything. He represents God to the world—divine presence embodied within human community. He achieves things far greater than any suffering-free fantasies or utopian views. Many gnostics want to free themselves from suffering, and in the process, they cause tremendous suffering for others. Some religions seek to free humankind from pain and death through committed indifference.

In recent years, I have realized that human suffering is actually something that connects the four culture spheres of science, ethics, the arts, and religion. This idea is worthy of a doctoral dissertation. We should be unafraid to talk about suffering and tragedy. Suffering and injustice connects with young people at a visceral and intellectual level; it resonates with their reality and sensibilities. Suffering hurts and it is sometimes terrible, confusing, and long-lasting. For Christianity, "Christ by taking on himself the world's guilt and sin on the cross, becomes the greatest proof that God is love. . . . The Cross is God's last word about himself."[51] Nothing in human experience is more profound than divine identification with our suffering: God allowed his Son to be sacrificed for fickle and rebellious human beings. It was a bodily death with real, excruciating pain and public humiliation. But this is precisely how God's *agape* love broke the back of sin, violence, and evil. He took the violence of the whole world upon himself on that Roman cross. He demonstrated dramatically how suffering can be redemptive, how it can improve and ennoble us. All the great biblical narratives come together in Jesus's great redemptive act: the return from exile, exodus from

49. Holland, *Dominion*.

50. Mongrain, *Systematic Thought of Balthasar*, 199.

51. Gawronski, *Word and Silence*, 180.

slavery, the great covenant stories, restoration of God's presence among his people, and finally his restorative justice. Israel's God returns in a dramatic fashion that fulfills deep Old Testament longings and promises.[52]

A powerful story acts like a good map. It helps us chart our course while simultaneously unlocking meaning and making sense of disparate ideas and experiences. There is commensurability amidst diversity. We see beyond the microscopic problems in our life, and grasp what really matters, what has *gravitas*.

> The Christian life involves re-understanding our entire lives and the whole world in the light of God's revelation. . . . Creation and covenant map our existence, and we need to learn how to read the maps and use a compass to find our way through the territory.[53]

Character begins to take shape in us as we struggle to face adversity, making our struggles a fruitful thing in the long run. Because of the incarnation, we are assured that we can find meaning in our suffering.[54] Suffering is necessary for maturity; suffering love is a mature phenomenon, moving us beyond self-interest. For example, a creative colleague of mine studying at Regent College, Dr. Laurel Borisenko, worked for the United Nations assisting African refugees. She discovered that theater presentations of their struggle connected them with a healing path. She helped them use their creative imagination to tell their stories of displacement, suffering, poverty, and violence. In each story, there are heroes and villains, but also promise and hope. By addressing our struggles courageously and wisely, we can move forward in gratitude and joy.[55] Suffering processed by placing ourselves in God's hands makes us more resilient. Connecting with the transcendent biblical story of long-suffering love, we are released from the dark victimhood to fate.

For the moment, let us focus on Jesus's post-resurrection presence. Beyond Jesus's profound embodied presence on earth, he has also been present in his community (John 14–17; Eph 4; Rom 12). As *agape* love incarnate, he left a following to carry this beautiful vision forward. He commissioned a mentored leadership—the apostles—to anchor us, and sent the Holy Spirit to guide us into all truth. This unique community of *called out ones* is a

---

52. Kaiser, *Promise Plan of God*.

53. Peterson, *Practice Resurrection*, 172.

54. Kreeft, *Making Sense Out of Suffering*.

55. Moltmann, *Theology of Hope*; Wright, *Surprised by Hope*.

historical and real extension of the incarnation. This diverse, worldwide community of Christians offers a cultural presence, performance, and embodiment of God's goodness and healing power around the globe. Over two billion people claim to be Christians today. It remains an influence of conscience and compassion, rights and justice for society. It promotes personal reform, recovery, and mature accountability. It does all this while feeding the starving and bandaging wounds, caring for creation, welcoming the refugee and practicing hospitality.

While it may not always be high profile, Christian involvement in the community at large has a profound and redemptive influence in many sectors of society, often at great personal cost to the believer. This entails a tremendous responsibility, opportunity, and benefit toward humanity. The high mandate of the faith is the flourishing of all, including a deep commitment to dialogue across various traditions—with a will to promote peace.[56] There is no room for racism among Christians. Genuine spiritual formation occurs within an environment of mutual, responsible relational connections, ones that make us whole. Missioned disciples spread not only the sayings but also the deeds and the incarnational *ethos* of Jesus. They authentically practice an ongoing miracle of self-sacrifice, forgiveness, and grace, while rejecting hate, vengeance, and violence. Christian community, while not perfect, is the active verb of God's presence, the Deed-Word, the *shalom* of God living out the drama of his love in concrete ways.

Impressively, there are in fact over one thousand verses of Judeo-Christian Scripture dedicated to concern for the poor and marginalized. That ought to catch our attention—God is very clearly a friend to the poor, as American justice activist Jim Wallis advocates.[57] One is reminded of that incredible speech by Portia in the Shakespeare's play *Merchant of Venice* concerning a defense of the quality of mercy. She claims that it makes us more human, closer to the divine. And so it does: compassion towards the other is an important matter of moral and spiritual *weight*. A famous saying by Mother Teresa of Calcutta put it poignantly: "The greatest evil is the lack of love and charity, the terrible indifference towards one's neighbor who lives at the roadside assaulted by exploitation, corruption, poverty and disease." Moral growth and stature of character develop through careful and consistent service to others, striving to exemplify the divine presence in our lives, the presence of Christ. The gospel calling is precisely this kind

56. Volf, Flourishing; Sachs, *Dignity of Difference, Not in God's Name.*

57. Wallis, *(Un)Common Good.*

of community, this kind of redemptive narrative. This is something worthy of building a whole life upon, something worth preserving as a dynamic in society.

We now want to discuss the move from community to communion: "I in them and you in me—so that they may be brought to complete unity. Then the world will know that you have sent me and have loved them even as you have loved me" (John 17:23). This state of being is reached as we dwell together in love and harmony, reflecting the unity of the Godhead through the Spirit of Christ living within us. Jesus's prayer is located at the very heart of God's superabundant grace. For two thousand years, it has been a journey for millions who wanted to become like Christ—to be in communion and loving relationship with God as Trinity. We continue this noble quest, listening to God's Spirit, asking him to know us, to reveal our false motives and attitudes in the process. This unity amidst diversity is a powerful apologetic to a watching world.

> To say that I am made in the image of God is to say that love is the reason for my existence, for God is love. Love is my true identity. Selflessness is my true self. Love is my true character. Love is my name. If, therefore, I do anything or think anything or say anything or know anything that is not purely for the love of God, it cannot give me peace, or rest, or fulfilment, or joy. To find love I must enter into the sanctuary where it is hidden, which is the mystery of God.[58]

We have a strong biblical source in the book of Philippians chapter 2: seeking unity (vv. 1–4); model of humility and sacrifice (vv. 5–11); pursuit of holiness (vv. 12–18). It offers an archetype of communion. Human unity naturally operates within the context of community—under the spirit of seeking the good of others in the communion of believers. Made in the image of God, we intuitively sense a feeling of solidarity as we come together in cooperation through spiritual friendship, witness, and worship. We also gain insight into the being of God as Trinity: *three-ness* and *one-ness*. The journey toward communion is sometimes long and arduous, but also deeply exciting, full of wonder and never-ending surprises.

My wife remembers well the breakthrough in her story of reconnecting with relatives behind the Iron Curtain. Through her visits there with her mother, alienation melted into love, joy, and the kindest community. Her family celebrated together when *the Wall* eventually came down in

---

58. Merton, *New Seeds of Contemplation*, 60, 61.

1989 as the Soviet Union crumbled and the two Germanies finally reunited in 1990 under Helmut Kohl. Prior to this, families were painfully divided and stifled. The motto of that era was this: Trust no one because your life and safety depends on it. How do people rediscover their spiritual imagination once again, experience re-enchantment, in a cynical age? How do we practice this amidst secularism the ideology, scientism, New Atheism, the Neo-Marxist Left, autocratic governments, Fascism, Stalinism, Maoism, rationalism, relativism, and consumerism? These are tough questions that challenge us deeply, but often lead to creative thought and wonderful initiatives.

In John 17:20, the text reflects Jesus's heart for the power of communion between heaven and earth: "My prayer is not for them alone. I pray for those who will believe in me through their message." Because Christ's actions are always consistent with the will of his Father, his prayer is destined to reach its creative fulfillment. He himself has introduced the way of unity by praying for us and modeling self-sacrifice. Our deep and real union with Christ is a taste of his union with the Father. This relationship within the Trinity is a beautiful model for human communion. It breaks down barriers in a way that is captured by theologian Christoph Schwöbel:

> It is one of the implications of this trinitarian conception of divine agency that the intentionality of divine action is not to be inferred from the structure of the world God has created, but has to be understood as grounded in the revelation in the Son. It is this paradigmatic action that is authenticated by the inspiration of the Spirit which then provides the framework for the interpretation of God's work in creation. In a similar way, the inspiration work of the Spirit indicates how God involves human beings in the realization of his intentions. It is the context of the interrelatedness of creation, revelation and inspiration that we can talk about God's action in terms of free, intentional action.[59]

Jesus beautifully reveals this dynamic oneness in the incarnation. Beyond our clan, family, or tribe, we have this God-given reality to fervently explore our quest for community and communion. The desire for unity, demonstrated by years of tears and repentance, is captured by Paul's words in Eph 2:14–15: "For he himself is our peace, who has made the two groups one and has destroyed the barrier, the dividing wall of hostility. . . . His purpose was to create in himself one new humanity out of the two, thus

---

59. Schwöbel, "God's Goodness and Human Morality," 70.

making peace." Paul was making reference to alienated Jews and gentiles in the ancient Greco-Roman world being offered one communion in Christ. Charles Taylor puts it brilliantly:

> Our being in the image of God is also our standing among others in the stream of love, which is that facet of God's life we try to grasp, very inadequately, in speaking of the Trinity. Now it makes a whole lot of difference whether you think this kind of love is a possibility for us humans. I think it is, but only to the extent that we open ourselves up to God, which means in fact, overstepping the limits set by Nietzsche and Foucault.[60]

Incarnation and redemption have opened the gate to mature unity amidst difference. This is depicted majestically by the poem in Phil 2.

Permit me one final note on healthy community and the road to re-enchantment. It is enhanced immeasurably by healthy, consistent spiritual practices. These practices, which are also called spiritual disciplines, include the inward disciplines of meditation, prayer, fasting, and study. The outward disciplines are simplicity, solitude, submission, and service. The corporate disciplines are confession, worship, guidance, and celebration. See Richard Foster, *Celebration of Discipline*;[61] Ruth Haley Barton, *Sacred Rhythms*;[62] Dallas Willard, *The Divine Conspiracy*;[63] and Don Postema, *Space for God*[64] for a good selection of spiritual writers. Spiritual disciplines help to heal and reintegrate our lives, set new direction. See the broad range of resources in my book, *Mapping the Future: Arenas of Discipleship and Spiritual Formation*.[65] Another key aspect of spiritual practice is stewardship, care for creation or earth care. Two splendid authors and rich thinkers that I have personally appreciated on this topic are Wesley Granberg-Michaelson and Steven Bouma-Prediger.[66]

In this chapter, we have discovered how important community and narrative are to a strong identity and to stable mental and spiritual health. It is delightfully countercultural to pursue community and communion in an

---

60. Taylor, *Catholic Modernity?*, 35.

61. Foster, *Celebration of Discipline*.

62. Barton, *Sacred Rhythms*.

63. Willard, *Divine Conspiracy*

64. Postema, *Space for God*.

65. Carkner, *Mapping the Future*.

66. Granberg-Michaelson, *Worldly Spirituality*; Bouma-Prediger, *For the Beauty of the Earth*.

age of radical individualism, fragmentation, entitlement, or even nihilism and war. We must work on it intentionally and consistently. Our story of incarnational spiritual culture is turning out to be richer and more exciting than we could have imagined. We will now see in our final chapter how the transcendent, infinite goodness can be mediated through this community of faith into society at large. This journey into the heart of reality requires dedicated human commitment combined with much divine grace. There are many treasures to be discovered for those with imagination, perseverance, and passion to follow through with this journey.

5

Transcendent Goodness
Meets the Good Society

IT SEEMS WISE TO start this chapter with a discussion of the philosophical issues surrounding the challenging categories of transcendent and
immanent with the help of philosopher Calvin Schrag.[1] Our focus here
is on *strong* transcendence, the possibility of an encounter with the *radically other*. It involves an epiphany that plays a role in human experience
and personal transformation. Strong transcendence impacts the process
of spiritual identity formation through discourse, action, perception,
and communal involvements. This impact occurs within all four culture
spheres: the arts, ethics, science and religion. Kierkegaard reveals its character through movement upward from the aesthetic to the ethical, and then
to the religious. This movement towards spiritual maturity occurs without
denying the value of the previous levels or the entwinement of all three. As
one moves upward, so to speak, one relativizes the level below but does not
eliminate it or make it irrelevant. It does, however, change its priority.

Another important distinction in Kierkegaard's thinking is between
Religiousness A and *Religiousness B*. Religiousness A speaks of the insti-
tutionalized aspects of religion within the immanent frame, within the
religious culture sphere. Religiousness B speaks of the profound encounter
with the radically transcendent Other (God), punctuated by the incursion
of the eternal into the temporal (incarnation, epiphany), informed by the

---

1. Schrag, *Self after Postmodernity*, 110–21.

descent of the transcendent into the historical life of the subject—into historical becoming. Some people never make it beyond Religiousness A. Note that Kierkegaard uses the grammar of *paradox* (faith) which is required for Religiousness B. In this level of experience, there is an impactful *transcendent dimension of depth*. This background is very important to our immediate discussion of how transcendent goodness can be mediated into the immanent world, in and through corruptible human nature. What exactly is the interface? Charles Taylor uses the term *epiphany* for such transformative encounters between the human and the divine realm. Throughout this book, we have been asking, "How can something historical become decisive for eternal happiness or wellbeing?" It provides a narrative of how that which is wholly other can impact our lives here and now, that which is beyond the immanent culture spheres, but still efficacious within them. The transcendent (God's speech) is not incommensurable with the immanent frame (human ears and lives), but does transcend it in important ways. There is no fundamental, incommensurable barrier between them, but they are quite distinct.

How does *radical alterity* (a term from Emmanuel Lévinas) impact human life according to our philosopher? How do we balance unity and diversity?[2]

1. Radical alterity offers a standpoint for critique, restraint, and vigilance. Further, it allows for an evaluation of beliefs and practices within the four culture spheres. This standpoint does not allow hegemony by any individual sphere, but relativizes them, while concurrently taking each one seriously as dimensions of lived experience. "Transcendence provides the requisite safeguards against ideological hegemony."[3] Science tends to be hegemonic in the early modern outlook—it becomes an ideology called *scientism*.[4] Aesthetics tends to become hegemonic in philosophers like Foucault and many other late moderns, rooted in Post-Romantic thought. This leads into the ideology of the aesthetic.[5] Radical alterity is a good defense against such extremes.

2. Schrag, *Self after Postmodernity*, 124, 128, 135.

3. Schrag, *Self after Postmodernity*, 124.

4. Hart, *Experience of God*.

5. Eagleton, *Ideology of the Aesthetic*. He is very insightful on Nietzsche and Foucault.

2. Radical alterity supplies conditions for the unification (but not an absolute state of unity) of the culture spheres. *Transversality* is the term Schrag uses, meaning a unification across difference and diversity. This is not universality, necessity, or identity. Instead, Schrag uses the term transversality as opposed to universality.[6] It involves more of an open textured process of unification rather than a state of being (absolute unity). But, neither does it entail pluralism or relativism on the other extreme. He uses the metaphor of the spine and the rib cage: distinctions with linkage.

3. Radical alterity provides resources for the transfiguration of the dynamics of self and societal formation: "The grammar of paradox, occasioned by the particularity of the Incarnation of the divine in the human, the incursion of eternity into the temporal and historical becoming, points beyond the economies of the culture-spheres, which remain beholden to the metaphors of production and consumption, distribution and exchange."[7] Thus, the self must go through a reconfiguration through its epiphanic encounter with radical alterity. This is a key insight into the transformational aspect of incarnational spiritual culture, with its trajectory of re-enchantment.

Finally, we also need a clear distinction between good and evil as background for our discussion in this chapter. Many are unclear or ambivalent about this distinction, they want to avoid it at all cost, thinking one person's good is another person's evil. Much confusion exists about these categories. But, we must work to transcend this fear to fully understand the meaning of both good and evil. French political philosopher Chantal Delsol understands our cultural ambivalence and yet brilliantly distinguishes the two clearly and insightfully in a way that resonates:

> Delsol's Definition of Evil: The Greek concept of *diabolos* literally means "he who separates," he who divides through aversion and hate; he who makes unjust accusations, denigrates, slanders; he who envies, admits his repugnance. The absolute Evil identified by our contemporaries takes the form of racism, exclusion or totalitarianism. The last in fact appears to be the epitome of separation, since it atomizes societies, functions by means of terror and denouncement, and is determined to destroy human

6. Schrag, *Self after Postmodernity*, 128.
7. Schrag, *Self after Postmodernity*, 135.

bonds. Apartheid and xenophobia of all varieties are champions of separation.[8]

Delsol's Definition of the Good: For contemporary man, the notions of solidarity and fraternity, and the different expressions of harmony between classes, age groups, and peoples, are still associated with goodness. The man of our time is similar to the man of any time insofar as he prefers friendship to hate and indifference, social harmony to internal strife, peace to war, and the united family to the fragmented family. In other words, he seeks relationship, union, agreement, and love, and fears distrust, ostracism, contempt, and the destruction of his fellow men. . . . The good has the face of fellowship, no matter what name it is given, be it love, the god of Aristotle, or the God of the Bible.[9] The certitude of the good finds its guarantee in the attraction it induces. The separation of the *diabolos* occurs constantly, but one day or another it will be pursued by mortal shame.[10]

PART I. AN INQUIRY CONCERNING INCARNATE TRINITARIAN GOODNESS

I have already broached the subject of incarnational presence in an earlier chapter. Now I will strive to define that presence in terms of *goodness*. I enlist the aid of two brilliant contemporary theologians, D. Stephen Long and Christoph Schwöbel. They offer a rich and pertinent articulation of the idea of a *transcendent turn to divine goodness*. Their work on the interface between divine and human goodness (transcendence and immanence) has significant resonance with Calvin Schrag and Chantal Delsol. Charles Taylor's trajectory for cultural and identity renewal emerges through a transcendent turn to *agape* love.[11] It will help to define more fully the character of such transcendence and the concept of the *epiphanic* encounter. At one level, *agape* is a quality of human relationships. It acts as a *hypergood* that informs and even organizes the other goods within one's moral horizon. Consequently, it both nuances and clarifies our perspective on human and divine goodness—*agape* is the river that runs our discourse.

8. Delsol, *Icarus Fallen*, 61.

9. Delsol, *Icarus Fallen*, 61–62.

10. Delsol, *Icarus Fallen*, 63.

11. Taylor, *Sources of the Self*, ch. 24, "Epiphanies of Modernism," pp. 456–94.

Notwithstanding, *agape* at another level can also be seen as animating and empowering the moral subject—it acts as a *constitutive good* rooted in transcendent divine goodness. *Constitutive* speaks of moral-spiritual-identity sources. The constitutive good, a category of moral motivation, gives meaning to and empowers the *hypergood* (one's dominant inspirational ideal or driver) and the other life goods within the moral frame. It provides the constitutive ground of the worth or value of the life goods, and allows the self to live the good life, to flourish morally. Moral identity is interwoven with the pursuit of the good in life within Charles Taylor's anthropology. It is the type of good that provides enabling conditions for the realization of *strong qualifications* in one's life. These are *qualities of the will* impacting the choices we make. Therefore, one's relationship to such a good is vital to building moral capacity for individuals and communities with a view to freedom and creativity. Knowing such a good personally also means loving it, wanting to act in accord with it, and growing toward it. Crucial to the position of the constitutive good is that it has independence from the self, with a level of objectivity. As Charles Taylor once put it to me in an email, "A constitutive good is a term I used for what I also called moral sources, something the recognition of which can make you stronger or more focused in seeking or doing the good. It's a matter of motivation and resilience, and not just a definition of your moral position."

I now pursue further understanding of *transcendent goodness*, and its implications for the healthy individual agent. There is a certain *strangeness* to the idea of transcendent divine goodness. Its radical alterity exceeds one's human cognitive grasp, or ability to define it, or at least to contain it. One can use terms like infinite, excellent, most intense, purest, unfathomable, or superlative as adjectives to describe this goodness. One cannot, however, fully grasp the qualitative dimensions of transcendent divine goodness with descriptors alone. It is truly *radically other*, and trans-historical. But of course with the incarnation, it gets embedded and revealed in human history and culture. In one sense, it is incompatible with human concepts of the good, but is not incommensurable. Thus, we experience a creative tension. Divine goodness is *infinitely* good (qualitatively) compared to human goodness. It blows the mind when we contemplate it and it brings us into deep humility and awe. Many great saints down the centuries have sat dumfounded in its presence, completely silenced. It is no mere human projection—the goodness that we find in the world points to and participates in, but is not identical with, the goodness, holiness, or righteousness that is God. This is an important starting point, a discourse that we find throughout Scripture.

By definition, transcendent goodness is much more than an absolute or a highest principle. We cannot reduce it to Kant's moral imperative, or a utilitarian good. Goodness is of *the very essence* of God. The claim that *God is good* entails a distinctive character trait predicate. Stephen Long attempts such an articulation when he writes: "God is good in the most excellent way."[12] This means that there can be no greater good, nor a position of goodness from which to judge God—another very significant point. There is no gnostic higher moral vantage point above God. This is a qualitative transcendence that is completely worthy of our love and admiration (the best, most beautiful, most excellent goodness). This theological viewpoint is particularly endemic to the poetry of the book of Psalms. God is the *gold standard* by which all human currencies of the good are measured. Put another way, there is an *irreducible density* to God's goodness; it has tremendous moral weight.

Christoph Schwöbel proceeds logically and profoundly from this perspective to say that in creation:

> God has set the conditions for being and doing the good and for knowledge of the good in the human condition. On this account, transcendent divine goodness is the ontological ground of the human good; the human moral horizon is rooted in God, contextualized by God, not vice versa. Furthermore, the knowledge of the good is intimately linked with the knowledge of God, and one's relation to the good is ultimately connected to one's relationship to God.[13]

One cannot conjure such goodness; it exists prior to human existence. D. Stephen Long adds further important texture to the distinction between human and divine goodness:

> Participation in God is necessary for the good and for freedom. Evil arises when freedom is lost through turning towards one's own autonomous resources for ethics. The fall does not result from people seeking to be more than they are capable of through pride but from their becoming less than they could be because they separate the knowledge of the good from its true end, God, and find themselves self-sufficient. . . . Seeking the good through

12. Long, *Goodness of God*, 21.
13. Schwöbel, "God's Goodness and Human Morality," 72.

nonparticipation in God, through the "virtue of what was in them-selves" makes disobedience possible.[14]

The religious and ethical spheres overlap here. This is what Long refers to as the *blasphemy of the a priori*. It is defined as the philosophical preoc-cupation and presumption that assumes one can determine the conditions for knowledge of the good, by oneself (*a priori*). Can we invent the good ourselves, subjectively? This idea assumes that one can do this without en-gaging goodness at its *best*—which is found solely in God. This is what Sam Harris is attempting in his popular book *The Moral Landscape*.[15] He attempts, but fails, to show a viable scientific foundation of the good. This would entail that rational scientists are the source of the good. James Da-vison Hunter and Paul Nedelisky respond with a brilliant critique of this posture.[16] This is a working assumption in Michel Foucault's moral self-making and reflexive self-love discussed in chapter 4. If the individual is the origin of the moral life, ethics would tend to be reduced to anthropol-ogy (what a tribe or king decides) or autobiographic projectionism (what I decide as values for myself).

Another insight that can be drawn from the loftier premise of tran-scendent goodness is that this divine goodness is—fortunately for all concerned—beyond human control, manufacture or manipulation. In the human world, it constitutes no mere social, legal, or governmental con-struction of the good. Human attempts to articulate the good, construct the good, or to be good, are only vague, finite, and inadequate facsimiles of God's goodness. This is what we mean by Christlikeness: we model ourselves af-ter, or mirror, his exemplary life and ethos. Humans are never the ultimate standard, despite the recognition that this is unknown to or unaccepted by many. These immanent articulations are also vulnerable to manipulation and exploitation, conflict of interpretations, and power interests. Foucault clearly understood this in his work on Power-Knowledge, his middle peri-od. This kind of manipulation is what incurs cynicism about the very use of the language of the good in our current cultural condition.[17] Some human standards are even tribal or historically contingent (Fascism), or a product of corrupt self-interest by those in power (populism), employed in coercive or abusive ways. They are employed arbitrarily by ideological leadership

14. Long, *Goodness of God*, 128.

15. Harris, *Moral Landscape*.

16. Hunter and Nedelisky, *Science and the Good*.

17. Delsol, *Icarus Fallen*.

on the right as well as the left. Human claims and social constructions of the good are necessary, but not sufficient. These contingent positions may offer a position from which to dialogue, but they are not the final word. There is a critical need for a transcendent divine goodness standard from above to arbitrate and critique various human claims to the good as well as human social constructions of the good. This parallels Calvin Schrag's idea of *strong transcendence* and *radical alterity* which was outlined at the outset of the chapter.

Furthermore, from a Christian worldview perspective, this strong transcendent goodness is *trinitarian and relational*. In other words, it is an intensely personal goodness of a tri-personal God (Father, Son and Holy Spirit). This transcendent goodness begins and is sourced in God. Only then does it flow to creation as generous gift, or as a *real presence* in the world. But how does this transcendence connect or sustain a relationship to the immanent world?[18] The answer is that they are distinct, but not completely separate. While communicable, the understanding and experience of goodness involves a journey towards the triune God amidst the divine journey towards the human race, including the invitation to dialogue—a theme which occurs throughout the entire Scriptural corpus. God's goodness is active in the world. This occurs through various revelations: Creation and Scripture, but supremely in the incarnation of Jesus Christ and the church he left as his witness on earth, a community now linked to transcendent goodness. The incarnation contains the best information and manifestation on the embodied goodness of God within the immanent frame, our time-space-energy-matter-human world.

A full defense of trinitarian theology of goodness is beyond the scope of this book. Instead, we will limit the discussion to the exploration of what trinitarian goodness looks like as a *plausibility structure*. I mean plausibility in the *strong* sense. This will enhance our understanding greatly, offering us a better articulate grasp of the human-divine relationship of ethics and spiritual development. I will do this by an analysis of *agape*, the gift of hospitality, and finally a look at the Holy Spirit as the mediator of divine goodness, both now and in future. Within this plausibility structure, the task of ethics is to then assist the individual in the journey from human nature as it stands to a higher moral vision and horizon. This *nature* includes its inclination toward the good but its lack of substantive context, its lack of robust moral source, and thus its temptation toward evil, selfishness, harm,

18. Gordon Carkner, "Charles Taylor and the Myth."

and violence—the lowest moral source. The critical move in this context is towards the concrete embodiment of what the individual can become in an intimate experience of and relationship with God's goodness.

As rooted in the Trinity, this transcendent horizon of infinite goodness involves the dynamic action of all three persons of the Christian Trinity in the world: incarnationally, existentially, and sometimes mysteriously. It is important to re-emphasize that the incarnation is grounded in the nature of God, not in the nature of humanity. It is a strong benefit, a gift, that human goodness can be evaluated in the light of divine goodness rather than in avoidance of it. According to this theological premise, "the trinitarian action in creation, revelation and inspiration in the world is all part of the moral horizon in which human moral reflection occurs."[19] The transcendent, radical alterity is effective and influential in the immanent culture spheres. It entails significant benefits for the human moral-spiritual-communal-narrative. This goodness is communicated through creation represented by the Father, through the Son, the God-man, in the incarnation. It is then communicated by the Holy Spirit as the source of empowerment and inspiration of human morality, starting with the Christian community and then radiating out from it. The three persons create the conditions for knowing and doing the good.[20] The Father as Creator has established the order and the possibility of goodness in his creation, a vital relational structure of goodness. He created both a moral and good world at once, one designed to promote human flourishing through cooperation with divine goodness. Therefore, he knows best what will help us flourish in daily life.

The Son, Jesus Christ, is the complete earthly revelation of divine goodness: "The Son is the radiance of God's glory and the exact representation of his being, sustaining all things by his powerful word" (Heb 1:3). The Hebrew prophets in their time underlined the word of God; he was the divine Word. Jesus represents a dramatic opportunity to see, encounter, and experience God's goodness within the human sphere—the definitive articulation of divine goodness within human culture and history. Immanence meets transcendence profoundly in the person of Jesus of Nazareth. The Spirit is the inspiration and motivation to integrate goodness into our lives. He offers gifts and superabundant graces—the fruits of the Spirit. He is a key source of the good for both individual and communal life. This is

---

19. Schwöbel, "God's Goodness and Human Morality," 71.
20. Schwöbel, "God's Goodness and Human Morality," 73.

how we can become morally good and grow into divine goodness or holiness. This involves transfiguration of our moral outlook and our motivations within all the culture spheres in which we operate. The Holy Spirit is in the business of transforming individuals, groups, and institutions to be more like God. He leads them into all truth, holiness, and integrity.

This articulation shows key ways by which finite humans can be drawn into the transcendent relationship to infinite goodness, through covenant. This makes divine goodness accessible and efficacious within the realm of human experience, yet without being assimilated into, or reduced to, the human realm. That is an important qualification: Divine agency is essential to healthy human agency. According to Christoph Schwöbel,

> It is one of the implications of this trinitarian conception of divine agency that the intentionality of divine action is not to be inferred from the structure of the world God has created, but has to be understood as grounded in the revelation in the Son. It is this paradigmatic action that is authenticated by the inspiration of the Spirit which then provides the framework for the interpretation of God's work in creation. In a similar way the character of the work of the Spirit as inspiration indicates how God involves human beings in the realization of his intentions. It is the context of the interrelatedness of creation, revelation and inspiration that we can talk about God's action in terms of free, intentional action.[21]

This leaves us in a state of awe. Transcendent trinitarian goodness is both secure and relevant because it resides in the integrity of trinitarian relationality, or the benevolent sociality and communion within God as three persons (*perichoresis*). In light of this, it becomes readily accessible and real within human existential experience. Creation, revelation, and inspiration are the combined work of the Trinity. This means that Taylor's *transcendent turn* to a greater horizon of the good (*agape* love) is no fantasy, but has strong viability. It makes a real difference. Thus, trinitarian incarnational spiritual culture provides a compelling plausibility structure, which works to strengthen one's identity into something robust: relational, loving, receptive, reflective, with strong agency. It opens the horizon of human experience towards a self with a transcendent dimension of depth (a *thick* self). "Blessed are those who hunger and thirst for righteousness, for they will be filled" (Matt 5:6).

21. Schwöbel, "God's Goodness and Human Morality," 70.

PART II. *AGAPE* LOVE REVEALS DIVINE GOODNESS IN REAL TIME

This discussion now leads us to analyze *agape* love as an elaboration of the impact of trinitarian goodness. *Goodness* is one of the strongest human longings. Who would deny that more love, joy, peace, patience, kindness, goodness, and self-control would improve our world and our experience of life? To begin, we must ask the question: What are the implications of the transcendent turn to *agape* love in further substantiating the case for transcendent goodness as a viable source of identity, and also a positive source for cultural inspiration? The triune God is a lively relation of three persons. Human and divine realities are dialogically connected. It is God's calling of the individual into relationship that gives her uniqueness. The I-Thou relationships within the Trinity find their epiphany in the I-Thou between God and humanity, immanently expressed within human history. Raymond Gawronski captures this beautifully:

> In the relation of God and humanity, it is the unlimited "I" of God that calls the limited "I" of humankind into existence. To be human means to be addressed by God in the word, and to be so created in the image of God, that one can receive the word and answer the word.[22]

But how can Christian leaders encourage real character depth in those they serve through spiritual formation, to move people beyond transactional, consumer-oriented spirituality? Consumer spirituality, as well as health and wealth gospels, set people up for recruitment by cults and greedy pyramid schemes. How do we protect individuals from imploding into a technological social media matrix, or from being weaponized for nefarious populist political purposes? Corruption and temptation surrounds us. In this darkness, the church needs resilient believers to live consistently, to shine a powerful light into culture. They are people who view creation and the world through the prism of the Trinity, the cross, and the resurrection. They see sacrifice for the other as a noble aspiration and a holy calling. Christians need wise guidance and ongoing discipleship to avoid destructive entanglements. In solidarity with Christ, they can be empowered to cultivate a life of love, to create space for God and others. The mandate we have discovered under the banner of incarnational spiritual culture is the mediation of God's presence and goodness within the human social

---

22. Gawronski, *Word and Silence*, 142.

matrix. The very meaning of life becomes service to the other, being-with-the-other, walking alongside the drug addict, the socially marginalized, or handicapped. There is no question that upon giving of oneself sacrificially, employing one's giftedness for the common good, it is more natural to discover the deeper joy and purpose of life. *Agape* is a deep well that does not run dry because it is sourced in the infinite God. We often meet God in the eyes of a person in need.

As James Davison Hunter says, we need to cultivate an *incarnational hermeneutic*. How do we make Christ as suffering servant known and present to the watching world? Eugene Peterson speaks up for trinitarian goodness as he creatively exposits the book of Ephesians in his thoughtful book on spiritual maturity and identity in Christ, *Practice Resurrection*:

> In the three persons, there is a versatile and dynamic oneness, yet there are also roles and primary actions that proceed uniquely from Father, Son and Spirit. God the Father: God bringing everything into being and holding everything together by his word. God the Son: God entering our history, showing God in action in human terms that we can recognize, accomplishing salvation for all. God the Spirit: God present with and in us, inviting us, guiding and counselling us, wooing us into participation in all God's ways of being God. All these operations of God are in evidence as Paul directs and accompanies us in the process of growing up in Christ.[23]

In contrast to late modern forms of escapist thinking, Christianity is centered around obedience in holiness, growth in virtue. Understanding emerges through an embrace of Jesus's example and teaching—*faithful presence*.[24] This leads to a beautiful experience of personal liberation, resilience, integrity, and courage. This is what it means to trust one's life to God in Christian practice of Deed-Word, backing up our words with compassionate deeds.

The two great alternatives facing us today are either: a. Promethean arrogance; or b. the greatness of adventure in humble obedience represented so elegantly in Phil 2. Nietzsche saw the great divide as *Dionysus versus the Crucified*.[25] Paul shows us in Philippians that we must seek unity and therefore *descend* before we *ascend*, humble ourselves before a God

23. Peterson, *Practice Resurrection*, 197.

24. Hunter, *To Change the World*.

25. Girard, "Dionysius versus the Crucified."

who exalts us, builds us up through his grace. Love, truth, and obedience are utterly intertwined (John 14:21). Truth and spiritual freedom can only be discovered when obedience to Scripture (taking it seriously as God's will and voice) remains the protocol for action. We resonate with former Archbishop of Canterbury, Rowan Williams, who writes, "At its center and permeating its relationships is the conviction that truth can only be shown and spoken in compassion—attention to the other, respect for and delight in the other, and also the willingness to receive loving attention in return."[26]

What is this philosophical turn to love? We are claiming that people can be protected from their self-defeating fantasies, social media and video games escapism, disengagement, and isolation. They can be brought bodily into sacrificial community where individuals are loved and mobilized for the good and the glory of God. The marginalized discover a fresh human dynamic and learn the skills of listening, empathy, and patience. They learn practical, actionable behavior that is constructive and responsible. The passion of Christ is the ultimate statement that God is love at the core of his being. The cross is the unsurpassable goal of the incarnation, the final stop in the descent of the Son (Phil 2) into the veil of darkness. The *Logos* became flesh in the man Jesus—a selfless act to redeem mankind, to bring unity, and wholeness. Christ incarnate displays the amazing graciousness and self-giving character of the infinitely good transcendent God within our immanent frame.[27]

Christoph Schwöbel notes that divine goodness, a communion of love, "finds its social form in the community of believers as the reconstituted form of life of created and redeemed sociality."[28] His point is that this community is called to communicate, mediate, and live into its baptism, live into and mediate such divine goodness to a needy world. Believers are called to promote the virtues of charity, humility, forgiveness, reconciliation, peace, and mercy as a reforming influence in society. Award-winning historian Tom Holland documents how influential this has been through centuries past and continues to influence policy in the present.[29] He reminds us that the Christian imagination of *agape* love has been vital in shaping Western cultural values and eventually reforming a brutal, nihilistic Greco-Roman world. The old ethics of raw, greedy power acquisition and conquer or be

26. Williams, *Truce of God*, 123.

27. Taylor, *Secular Age*, 539–93.

28. Schwöbel, "God's Goodness and Human Morality," 76.

29. Holland, *Dominion*.

conquered barbarity of the ancient world is not the final word. Early Christians stood up to such violence of empire through a transcendent turn to divine goodness. They lived into their strong belief that love trumps power.

> The Son of God, by becoming mortal, had redeemed all humanity. Not as a leader of armies, not as the conqueror of Caesars, but as a victim, the Messiah had come. The message was as novel as it was shocking—and was to prove well suited to an age of trauma.[30]

One of the examples Tom Holland uses is that Christians adopted baby girls left to die on the trash heaps of the ancient world. Another is where they stayed in the cities during the plague and nursed suffering people. Every individual counted with them, they had dignity and worth. This became the headwaters and foundation stone of the human rights and freedoms that we enjoy today.

To demonstrate this point, the United Nations International Charter of Human Rights is a landmark statement on the value of each human being and how they ought to be treated. It draws philosophical nourishment from the incarnational spiritual culture. Charles Malik, former president of the United Nations General Assembly, was a key player in drafting the document and successfully obtaining a majority of signatory nations. This Lebanese philosopher was motivated by his Christian faith and his concern for justice and peace in the world after an immensely destructive World War II (1939–45) which was rooted in elitism, hate, revenge, and oppression. In 1948, Malik was elected president of the Economic and Social Council (ECOSOC), the Commission of Human Rights' parent body. Later that year, he chaired the third session of the UN General Assembly, which presided over the passage of the Universal Declaration of Human Rights (UDHR), and it was largely because of his diplomatic skills that it passed unanimously with only eight abstentions.

I remember well as a young campus chaplain Charles Malik's famous Pascal Lecture at the University of Waterloo: "A Christian Critique of the University." It is now published as a book.[31] Malik decried the attempts in higher education to sweep Christ's influence out of the modern university. Jesus's followers are thus called to halt the victimization of others and call the aggressors out on their bullying tactics.[32] They do not promote or

30. Holland, *Dominion*, 103.

31. Malik, *Christian Critique of the University*.

32. Volf, *Exclusion and Embrace*. This is a profound discourse on victimization and forgiveness.

tolerate social chaos, autocracy, or anarchy. Rather, Jesus's disciples endeavor to carve out a redemptive path in life: build for truth, justice, forgiveness, and reconciliation.

Goodness as we have defined it is *divine, transcendent, trinitarian goodness*, not an idealistic fantasy. It is rooted in reality; it carries serious moral weight and empowers people with vision for a better world. It offers a possible paradigm shift for many today—a high calling out of selfish individualism and narcissism. Jesus is the hermeneutic of a new, reconciled humanity, committed to the practice of forgiveness, gratitude, and peacemaking. Christopher Watkin captures its unique, exemplary thrust:

> Love is the epicenter of the distinctively Christian way of being in the world—not power, respect, or tolerance, not equality, justice, freedom, enlightenment, or submission. Love is the overall shape of Christian ethics, the form of human participation in the created order. . . . Love sets the rules for how that world is structured and functions in its entirety. . . . Love is a way of being in and experiencing the world, approaching friends and enemies alike as people to be loved. . . . It is the warp and woof of Christian relationships. . . . Love is the signature disposition of Christ's disciples.[33]

From the outside, this call may appear daunting or unrealistic. But we are never alone in this transformation process, as many others share our journey and support us. In community, people work as a team, receive guidance from others and learn how to share their own giftedness within the body of believers. *Gift* and *grace* in Christian community establishes a fresh interpretation of life that *goes all the way down*, fostering a new, delightful economy of grace. These gifts, this transcendent economy of superabundant grace makes life richer, full of wonder and meaning. That is the power of *agape* love. Charles Taylor hinted at this move in *Sources of the Self*, but became much more overt about the importance of such love in *A Secular Age*.

---

33. Watkin, *Biblical Critical Theory*, 390.

PART III. JESUS IS THE GOLD STANDARD OF INCARNATIONAL GOODNESS

Cultural nihilism[34] stands as a reductive, depersonalizing, disenchanted contrast to incarnational spiritual culture. The tone of nihilism is depicted clearly by the articulate Eugene Peterson:

> We depersonalize God to an idea to be discussed. We reduce people around us to resources to be used. We define ourselves as consumers to be satisfied. The more we do it, the more we incapacitate ourselves from growing up to a maturity capable of living adult lives of love, adoration, trust and sacrifice. . . . In our identity-confused society, too many of us have settled for a pastiche identity composed of social security number, medical records, academic degrees, job history, and whatever fragments of genealogy we can salvage.[35]

Surely we should not be satisfied with this kind of stripped-down identity. Within the incarnational community, human suffering, vulnerabilities, and alienation can be taken seriously and dealt with constructively. This is a countercultural move. Jesus is the faithful, consistent *imago Dei* accepting the prophetic mandate of the *Suffering Servant* spoken of by Isaiah (Isa 42:1–4; 49:1–6; 50:4–11; 52:13—53:12), the eighth-century BCE prophet. He is the servant who empathizes with our sorrow, pain, and vulnerabilities; he does not stand far off. He is the servant who suffers with us while confronting corruption, hypocrisy, and contemporary deconstructions of the human identity. The call of Abraham and of Israel as a nation was to become a generous blessing to the whole world—a conduit of grace and goodness. Millennial writer Jimmy Myers lucidly captures the point:

> He [Jesus] exemplifies and creates a people committed to what David Bentley Hart calls "strange, impractical, altogether unworldly tenderness" to those whom Nietzsche would have annihilated [and Hitler did]. . . . The beauty of this person, wholly man and wholly God, lies in the mystery that he brings salvation to the world not by excluding suffering but by uniting himself to it.[36]

This offers amazing insight. What emerges is the potential of discovering meaning in our suffering and our dying. Jesus's compassionate exemplum,

34. Carkner, *Great Escape from Nihilism*.

35. Peterson, *Practice Resurrection*, 66, 79.

36. Myers, "Is It True?"

his passion, is both public truth and moral resource. It becomes an inspiration to the incarnational community and to the larger human community. He pioneered a new way forward, modeled and mentored followers in the virtues, the spiritual graces and the spiritual imagination. A deeper awareness of suffering and tragedy is one means to unite the various human culture spheres (Schrag's *tranversality*). Suffering requires insight from all spheres (science, aesthetics, ethics, and religion) and contributes to them in turn. Transcendent divine goodness bridges—keeps in balance—what can seem in opposition. At the end of the day, Jesus is the glue to unite these spheres dynamically. Modern psychotherapy suggests that facing the dark side of ourselves, however painful, is a necessary part of the process of healing. It also leads to humility, one of the most important human virtues for growth in wisdom. A high view of Jesus believes him to work real miracles in a person's life: career, family, and church.

Permit me a further observation on Nietzsche: At the end of his life, Nietzsche realized that it came down to a critical choice between the Christ (suffering love) and Dionysus (self-indulgence and entitlement). But Nietzsche despised Christian *agape* love and the vulnerable concern for the weak and the victim.[37] Late moderns would do well to ponder the consequences of such a choice, as they continue to struggle through their own existential *angst*. Jesus's suffering is not weak, frustrating, or pathetic, but rather a highly redemptive love—*suffering-along-with-us*. His truth breaks the back of evil and helps to expose dark mechanisms and power game tactics in our politics and business, things such as weaponized lies, corruption and divisiveness. He is the ultimate victim who calls for an end to all victimization and violence against the neighbor (individual, national, and international). He is our champion, fighting on our side. Jimmy Myers captures it:

> He [Jesus] brings the whole festival of divine grace to a world that
> has excluded itself from it and invites.... humanity to take part, to
> enjoy a feast of resurrection where all divisions, segregation, and
> exclusion are transcended, where all have their place at the supper of the Lamb, where all, who see the face of the Beautiful One
> and in that seeing are transformed, are inundated and radiated by
> Beauty itself. In a word, to paraphrase St. Athanasius, he becomes

---

37. Hart, *Atheist Delusions*, 3–18. Nietzsche's gospel is radically opposed to the Christ.

the Ugly One so that we, the original ugly ones who have made this world ugly with our violence, might become beautiful.[38]

As depicted in the Sermon on the Mount (Matt 5–7), Jesus is a sign of divine anger against negative social conditions: exploitation, victimization, marginalization, and injustice. He was definitely a man of the common people, and a challenge to corrupt religious and governmental hierarchies. His countercultural stance was that the leader must be the servant of all, rather than the bully. It was very good news for those at the bottom of social hierarchies, but also a threat to those at the top of the power grid. Christopher Watkin calls it the *Great Reversal*.[39] At the beginning of Jesus's ministry, he proclaimed,

> The Spirit of the Sovereign Lord is on me, because he has anointed me to proclaim good news to the poor. He has sent me to proclaim freedom for the prisoners and recovery of sight for the blind, to set the oppressed free, to proclaim the year of the Lord's favor. (Luke 4:18–19; cf. Isa 61:1–2)

Most prophetic traditions have been concerned with justice for the poor, the neglected, homeless, and marginalized. Jesus models intolerance of evil and cruelty, opposing ideologies, institutions, and structures that seek to undermine human flourishing. He contends with those that seek to exploit or enslave the weak for personal gain. Moreover, he is against politicizing religion, against using public rage, victim rhetoric, and vice for the purpose of controlling the masses. David Bentley Hart makes an excellent case for the transformative power of Christian love in shaping history and institutions.[40] Jesus's life and witness sums up the whole of Scripture in love (Matt 22:35–40). Love sets the rules and parameters for a good and successful life. Love is the prime directive. This *agape* incarnational community provides a home (Luke 6), a safe space of refuge amidst the conflicts, tragedies, and transitions of life. Moreover, Jesus directly addresses the tectonic plate debates of our time—inequity, xenophobia, autocracy, poverty, manifold refugees, climate concerns, international debt, and terrorism.

The *agape* community offers a safe space where we can become *persons* in a fulsome sense. To illustrate, such a community can redirect our desires, bring peace instead of a sword, hope instead of despair, kindness

---

38. Myers, "Is It True?"

39. Watkin, *Biblical Critical Theory*, 379–89.

40. Hart, *Atheist Delusions*, ch. 12, "A Liberating Message," pp. 146–65.

instead of cruelty. Rowan Williams writes about reconciliation, "Peace does not come without integrity, wholeness of human desire."[41] Incarnate communal life therefore releases us from unconscious fear, anxiety, defensiveness, and the ingrained compulsions of rivalry. Living within such a communal life helps people grow in awareness of their vulnerability, interdependence, mutuality, and contingency. Jesus's followers, at their most authentic, work against injustice, violence, and exploitation. They resist evil where they are able. Christopher Watkin captures a key aspect of love in Christ, showing its wonderful relevance and complexity in light of God's goodness and generosity.[42]

> To love . . . is to renounce the freedom of being an island, of keeping one's options open. But love's open secret . . . is that there is a greater, richer freedom in the love relationship than could ever be experienced in the serial encounters of noncommitment. . . . Love always involves a willing enslavement, a form of self-disposession, or self-giving. . . . Biblical love and modern freedom-from are mutually exclusive modes of being in the world. . . . We are not forced to choose between freedom and love.[43]

In another striking example, Dr. Martin Luther King Jr. saw how the solidarity of mutual love could empower social change and call us to our better selves. He understood the critical testimony of the *Beloved Community* rooted in the ethics of nonviolence in the Sermon on the Mount. This kind of suffering love is depicted in the feature film on his life mission, *Selma*. It emerges from a deep faith and a vision of a benevolent God who believes in human dignity for all races. For King, as a daily experience, he and his colleagues risked their health and their lives for the vision of *agape* love together with a commitment to nonviolent justice. His dream continuously called people to the mountaintop of virtue, reconciliation, and hope. Christian activist Jim Wallis resonates with King's example of pro-active resistance to the forces of *diabolos*:

> When Jesus is asked by his disciples who will be first in his kingdom, he tells them it will be the servants of all. Humility is one of the most poorly appreciated values in our intensely competitive culture, economy and politics.[44]

41. Williams, *Truce of God*, 103.
42. Watkin, *Biblical Critical Theory*, 390–400.
43. Watkin, *Biblical Critical Theory*, 392–93.
44. Wallis, *(Un)Common Good*, 49.

One key historical marker for the inauguration of this new incarnational community is the resurrection of Jesus of Nazareth. UK Bishop Lesslie Newbigin appropriately called it a starting point, a *singularity* that cannot be explained by anything prior. It stands as a new beginning, a historical marker for humanity, and a brilliant hope for transformation, a significant cultural breakthrough. Articulate author Andy Crouch captures its profound historical and cultural impact—changing all the metrics of life:

> The resurrection was a culture-shaping event. . . . If indeed it happened as Jesus' followers proclaimed, [it] changed more of subsequent human history, for more people and more cultures, than any other event one can name. . . . The resurrection of Jesus is like a cultural earthquake, its epicenter located in Jerusalem in the early 30's [C.E.], whose aftershocks are being felt in the cultural practices of people all over the world, many of whom have never heard of, and many more of whom have never believed in, its origins. . . . The resurrection is the hinge of history—still after two thousand years as culturally far-reaching in its effects as anything that has come since.[45]

The incarnation, death, and resurrection of Jesus the Christ, the Son of God, is indeed a game changer, a vision-shaping event. Violence and evil can be vanquished. It calls us to a radical reassessment of how we discover our individual dignity, identity, spiritual and cultural wholeness. The incarnational spiritual culture provides a strong platform that can heal our divisions and set things on a new trajectory.

PART IV. THE HOLY SPIRIT AS A CONDUIT OF DIVINE GOODNESS

Now I want to discuss the growth in capacity of moral being. We often think too small and expect too little of God. I have already introduced the person of the Holy Spirit. Now let me elaborate on his contribution to incarnational spiritual culture. As the third person of the Trinity, the Holy Spirit is a vital part of the discussion of transferring divine goodness into the world, engaging culture creatively. Humans do not flourish by the example of Jesus alone. Too often, we easily become discouraged or guilt-ridden as we try to follow such a high model of human existence. What is the solution?

45. Crouch, *Culture Making*, 143, 145.

If goodness is a dynamic, mysterious gift, and cannot be achieved by human effort alone, even heroic human effort, from whence come the sources of the good? How is the quality of the human will actually enhanced in everyday *praxis*? Here's a key reminder from philosophical theologian James K. A. Smith:

> The Incarnation is the locus of God's self-revelation—the primary site of God's self-giving. Thus the logic of the incarnation is fundamentally an account of *what gives*, of how difference and otherness is revealed—whether that is the "horizontal" revelation of ourselves to one another or, paradigmatically, the revelation of divine transcendence in the region of immanence that is creation. Hence the logic of incarnation is an account of revelation.[46]

How then is goodness mediated through Taylor's transcendent turn towards *agape* love? Can the Holy Spirit extend the logic of the incarnation? Jesus, in fact, promised his disciples that he would send the Holy Spirit upon his ascension—to extend his work and mission, empower leadership to build his church. Clearly, there must be a source of empowerment for living in a positive, fruitful relationship to transcendent, trinitarian goodness. Otherwise, Christianity seems like an unattainable ideal. We need motivation for practicing the good, for self-sacrifice, for mediating such glorious goodness within society—the essential call of the *imago Dei*. We also seek personal transformation and change of vision. If one pursues it without divine help, does it not become impossible? In other words, is transcendent goodness so heavenly other that it is of no human good? What are the tangible, embodied, social, historical, human possibilities of exhibited goodness? We surely have a need to know because, as shown already, moral sources are spiritual gold.

With these questions in mind, it is crucial to remember that the Holy Spirit is a large inspirational and transformational factor in human goodness. Put another way, the Holy Spirit is necessary for the personal actualization of divine goodness. The Spirit is continuously at work amidst the historical contingencies of community development. This is pertinent to the logic of incarnation articulated by James K. A. Smith.[47] Incarnation does not stop with the life of Jesus the Jewish Messiah. Brilliant Duke University theologian D. Stephen Long is both realistic and optimistic about the human quest for the good and for sound reasons. He believes that with

46. Smith, *Nicene Option*, 201.

47. Smith, *Nicene Option*, 63–92.

the Holy Spirit, the third member of the Trinity, moral self-constitution can be intimately and fruitfully interfaced with the goodness of God. This can lead to personal and social transformation as incarnation is internalized in the lifestyle of Jesus's faithful followers. This in turn rejuvenates and prioritizes ethics and moral self-realization. It offers a reconstitution of both goodness and freedom. Long captures the concept:

> The Holy Spirit *infuses* a goodness into us that makes us better than we know we are by ourselves. This *better* is what theologians mean by *grace*. People find themselves caught up in a journey that results in the cultivation of gifts and beatitudes they did not know were possible. They discover that this journey was possible only through friendship. . . . The mission of the Holy Spirit is to move us towards the charity that defines the relationship between the Father and the Son, a charity so full that it is thoroughly one and yet cannot be contained within a single origin or between an original and a copy, but always, eternally, exceeds that relationship into another. The Holy Spirit is that relationship.[48]

I am arguing that divine goodness is made tangibly available as a *gift* by the Holy Spirit for the transformation and moral empowerment of the human individual and the church. Thereby, everyday broken human players have the potential to become *new creatures in Christ*. The Holy Spirit offers relationship and empowerment for existentially acting out and promoting the good, with a view to a more fair and just world. Christians can thus embody and become *entrepreneurs* of divine goodness via the empowerment of the Spirit through prayer and other spiritual practices. He is a key source of wisdom as the Spirit of Christ. There is both mystery and tangibility in this empowerment as philosophical theologian Anthony Thiselton explains below.

> This creativity, which transforms and reverses the passive situatedness of the postmodern self, becomes possible through the Holy Spirit because the Spirit transposes self-interest, conflict and bids-for-power into *love for others* (for individuals and groups) and *for the Other* (for God and whatever is not self). Hence the co-operative effects of the Holy Spirit and the cross of Christ together actualize God's self-giving *as God*. . . . Woven into logic of the work of Christ and the Spirit is the inter-personal, interactive

48. Long, *Goodness of God*, 302–3.

character of love. *Perichoresis* means the interpenetration, mutuality, co-sharing and loving reciprocity.[49]

Thiselton offers us a *tour de force*, demonstrating the vital nature of the Spirit's role. This is the profound impact of the *epiphanic* experience of *I-Thou* encounter that we spoke of earlier. The Holy Spirit is very central to the moral life, motivation, and moral sources: the Spirit *gifts* individuals for works they cannot imagine or achieve in their own strength. They cannot accomplish such feats within the limits of their own personal resources and human will alone. He transforms them and makes them capable of forgiveness, virtue, reconciliation, and love. This too is part of the miracle of the incarnation. He makes possible and effective the mission of the transformative goodness of Jesus Christ, both within and through his church—impacting culture at large. Ultimately, it gets public play within society and raises the bar of ethical standards. This empowers a person's faith and raises expectations, hopes, and vision for a better future. The Spirit calculates as the ongoing presence of Jesus in the church and in the world. The assembly of believers can thereby become the *faithful presence* of Christ, promoting this new culture of *shalom*. The Spirit entwines everyday human beings with the very life of God, and draws them into the communion of the Trinity. This is a profound realization.

This particular process of moral self-constitution and spiritual wholeness opens up the horizon of human moral thinking and praxis (*qualities of the will*), first towards God. Secondly, it connects the individual through compassion with other people's suffering, empowering them to move beyond raw self-interest into self-giving service—in forms of radical hospitality. Within the trinitarian goodness plausibility structure, we can begin to answer one of Charles Taylor's questions of the age: How can we sustain the Western societal *hypergood* of benevolence, human rights, and reduction of human suffering? To answer it, we remember that the Holy Spirit enriches, motivates, and empowers the individual and the incarnational community as the abundant and fecund connection to the highest source of divine goodness. That access is profound, riveting, a truly phenomenal promise. Resilience in living the good, promoting the good, comes through relationship with God the Holy Spirit and the regular exercise of this grace. Humans can be transfigured into something more beautiful.

D. Stephen Long adds an important insight to this discussion. Together with Christoph Schwöbel, he finds that the kind of ethics that

49. Thiselton, *Interpreting God and the Postmodern Self*, 154, 157.

emphasizes the will and absolute freedom of choice is poorly focused on a Dionysian release of the desires. This is not a trajectory of moral and social maturity, with mutual accountability. It leads to the dangerous human temptation to set one's own standard of goodness (*solipsism*), and to surreptitiously manipulate the language of the good in the direction of pure self-interest. Overweening self-will has too often led to conflict, corruption, and violence. Humans have a sad history of using their freedom for self-indulgence—in contradiction to God's culture of goodness. They coerce and deceive their neighbors, misrepresent the truth, or abuse the natural world by their own controlling interest in setting the standard of *moral currency*. So many dictators have longed to replace God in this manner, encouraging citizens to worship them and trust their policies. They attempt to set cultural norms and laws with a view to their own self-aggrandizement. They either live above the law, or become the law. Long and Schwöbel in contrast promote the idea that ethics should be focused on the constitution of the self as it relates dynamically, and embraces God and transcendent goodness as a moral *a priori*. This is parallel to the thought of Charles Taylor, who noted that the first question of ethics is "Who or what do you love?" James K. A. Smith follows this theme in his fine book, *You Are What You Love*.[50] He discusses the importance of regular spiritual practices, disciplines, and habits of the heart as a lifestyle. What are the habits of goodness that you are integrating into your daily routine?

The qualities of the will come into play at this juncture. D. Stephen Long believes that moral self-constitution must be rooted in a love of God: a love of the infinitely superior and pure goodness that is God. When we reflect on this infinite, wholly other goodness, it creates a sense of awe and gratitude. I remember personally feeling overwhelmed while first researching this concept of infinite divine goodness—I was brought to tears, humbled by a deep joy. How can we appropriate such goodness into our lives, even at the beginner level, taking a humble stance towards transformation? The desire to obey, to follow the path of goodness, increases as we cooperate with the Spirit, walk in step with the power of the Spirit. We will then delightfully see the gifts and the fruits of the Spirit emerge in our lives and our congregation. Thereby, we recognize that God is an infinite source of superabundant grace and love.

The picture of the lone individual will choosing between good and evil, or embracing both ambivalently in an aesthetic move of self-mutilation is

50. Smith, *You Are What You Love*.

deeply problematic. Humans simply do not have the fullest capacity within themselves. To grow into adulthood, for a social species like *homo sapiens*, one must not become autonomous, lonely, and solitary. Rather, it is to become a person of integrity—the one on whom others can depend. The ideology of the autonomous individual—making self the primary love of one's life—is a negative distraction from moving into the *goodness-which-is-God*. Stephen Long optimistically focuses on building one's life orientation, one's identity, one's lifestyle practices around divine goodness. This grounds our identity and life in Christ. Such goodness cannot be reduced to an achievement of the human will. We must receive it and be transformed by it first, as in the language of Kierkegaard's Religiousness B.

> Human freedom is not about the capacity to choose [merely] between good and evil. Human freedom occurs when our desires are so turned toward God and the good that no choice is necessary. . . . Jesus shows us that such a life is possible *in our humanity*—not against it.[51]

This simple posture towards God and the world can change the whole trajectory of our lives, reshape our goals, passions, and longings. Moral-spiritual-identity transformation comes through a commitment to the good, not through seeking a controlling knowledge (*gnosis*) of good and evil—thus trying to play God. This has always turned out badly. Nor does it come through creative strategies for mere self-control or manipulation of power relations and truth games (Foucault). Such an approach is a sign of despair as Kierkegaard signaled to his fellow Europeans. Human creatures as self-legislating, individualistic beings do not possess the moral resources to enact goodness *per se*, although they certainly try. Some people are decidedly nice and civil, even if they deny God's existence. They may even have a strong instinct for high moral values such as respect for others or human rights for the disadvantaged. But acts of the will do not automatically constitute acts of goodness; they may be mere self-justification, pride, or the easing of one's conscience. Dr. Long strongly underlines this idea as a philosophical floor in ethics: *Goodness is discovered in God*, it is not invented by the self. On the same trajectory as Charles Taylor, Long concludes that the primary question for the moral self is "What or who is the good I seek and that seeks me?"[52] It is personal, existential. This entails a

51. Long, *Goodness of God*, 46.
52. Long, *Goodness of God*, 130.

certain seriousness in the quest for the good that could become the passion and driving force of one's whole life. It is such a fundamental and fruitful question for self-examination and personal growth.

Schwöbel finesses the point further, summarizing brilliantly the thrust of our argument on effective mediation of divine goodness, moving us towards the gift of response and responsibility—high freedom:

> The reconstitution of created freedom through the appropriation of the revelation of God's goodness in Christ which is made possible in the Spirit is characterized by the acknowledgement of the limitations of human freedom that become evident where this freedom is no longer understood as self-produced, but as a gift of grace. The liberation from the abortive attempt of self-constitution of human freedom discloses the reality of the other person and the non-human creation as the one to whom good action is directed. Human goodness is realized where it is acknowledged that it is not self-produced, but the gift of God's creative, revealing and inspiring action.[53]

Through the Holy Spirit, this transcendent goodness that starts as a *radical alterity* becomes fully communicable, accessible, and transformative—lively and active within our communities of faith. The transcendent interfaces with the immanent in Christ and in us, the body of Christ. Thereby, the *imago Dei* is restored for humanity to reveal us as more like God's character, mirroring Christ to one another. In that sense, Jesus becomes the *New Adam*, the beginning of a new human community. It impacts and reshapes culture as Oxford professor Larry Siedentop writes in *Inventing the Individual*.[54] The individual is not left alone to her own devices and resources, to make her own way in the world. Nor does she need any longer to justify her bad behavior or live in anxiety, ambivalence, guilt, shame, and remorse.

The Holy Spirit connection between human goodness and the transcendent brings forward a robust hope for reviving culture, for renewed culture-making.[55] The resources for the good are superabundant, if we decide to seek them out. Furthermore, this is writ large in the poetry of Pss 90–103. The sheer majesty of the breathtaking goodness of God is revealed as powerful and transformative in the very fabric of people's lives and in creation. The poetics of these psalms are profoundly insightful regarding

53. Schwöbel, "God's Goodness and Human Morality," 75.

54. Siedentop, *Inventing the Individual*.

55. Crouch, *Culture Making*.

the human condition and how God fills the gap between divine and human realities. At the end of the day, we should remain skeptical regarding mere human constructions of the good. On this point, I agree with many late modern deconstructionists. But we must remain open to all that can be communicated about the goodness of the triune God through creation, Scripture, the incarnation, and the transforming work of the Holy Spirit. There is much to celebrate. The conversation about the good in moral discourse is revived as we experience personally the tangible *presence* of the life-transforming, divine goodness within New Covenant life. It has offered refreshment and a new beginning for so many weary travelers trying to find their way.

This is a paradigm shift compared to French philosopher Michel Foucault's stance which has garnered much influence in recent decades within the university and Western culture at large. He assumes that individual humans are the origin and controlling agents of moral currency and sees the moral agent through his ethics as aesthetics and the art of self. Carl R. Trueman offers us the historical background to this *Romantic Turn*, the contemporary reigning ideology of the aesthetic, in his masterful contribution, *The Rise and Triumph of the Modern Self*.[56] He notes about contemporary ethics within our social imaginary that "The expressive individual grants his own personal preferences the status of universal moral imperative."[57] Trueman's landmark analysis traces its development over two hundred years of Western cultural evolution to the dominant social and political assumptions of our day—the revolution of identity politics, where sexual identity is the key expression of personal identity. Here's how he articulates our cultural situation: "That society or nurture, is to blame for the problems individuals have in this world . . . is virtually an unquestioned orthodoxy, and it influences everything, from the philosophies of education to debates about crime and punishment."[58] It is also an anti-religious movement that trashes the sacred.

The moral self, in Foucault's view, seeks for autonomous resources (apart from God) in the pursuit of a radical freedom: self-control, self-expression, and self-construction. It entails one's total reinvention or self-creation, over against the world. In the dialogue between Foucault and Taylor in my doctoral dissertation, it does come down to a watershed between the *sovereignty of self* over against the *sovereignty of God* (infinite goodness),

56. Trueman, *Rise and Triumph*. A companion volume: Favale, *Genesis of Gender*.

57. Trueman, *Rise and Triumph*, 86.

58. Trueman, *Rise and Triumph*, 125.

my personal, asserted goodness versus God's goodness, the *telos* of self-interest versus the *telos* of generous divine, self-giving love. It makes a huge difference whether God and *agape* love are allowed to map one's moral and spiritual horizon. The posture of this book's discourse encourages love of self and love of the world (despite the evil inherent in that world and in oneself), brought together with an openness to the circulation of divine grace (Eph 3:14–19). Love and honor of God, however, remains our prime mandate. This is countercultural, incarnational spirituality at its most resilient and resourceful.

Thus, Charles Taylor's *transcendent turn to agape love* has proved a fruitful reflection that bears serious consideration for a dynamic, growing moral and spiritual identity—a good and robust future for the soul. We have a great opportunity ahead of us as we follow Jesus Christ into a new world that has been opened to us. There is much here to access and discover about the potential human state of affairs, particularly amidst our current cultural revolution. In *Strengthening the Soul of Your Leadership*, Ruth Haley Barton has a wonderful chapter on the longing for a strong sense of God's goodness as leaders.[59] It includes a meditation on Moses's dilemma of leadership amidst a feeling of deep existential loneliness and inadequacy. He perceived that his call to free Israel from Egypt during the Exodus, crossing a vast desert, involved an impossible, humanly overwhelming task. It has become the greatest symbol of salvation and liberation in the entire Bible, apart from Calvary:

> God knew that what Moses most needed to see and what would sustain him for the long haul of leadership was a glimpse of God's goodness and mercy. "I will make all my goodness pass before you, and will proclaim before you the name, 'The Lord'; and I will be gracious to whom I will be gracious, and will show mercy on whom I will show mercy." (Exodus 33:17–19) God's goodness is his greatest glory and it is what we most need.[60]

Moses emerged from this epiphany a changed man due entirely to his mountaintop experience of epiphanic encounter with glorious, divine goodness in the cleft of the rock on Mount Sinai. He consequentially became a renewed, courageous, and focused leader who was in synchrony with his calling. The church at its most authentic today is a community that majors on entering deeply into God's goodness. It then joyfully transmits

59. Barton, *Strengthening the Soul*, 155–67.
60. Barton, *Strengthening the Soul*, 161.

that goodness to a needy world. That is our calling as an incarnational spiritual culture that is grounded in Christ. As Christ's representatives on earth, the contemporary church produces people on a dedicated, heroic quest for such goodness. Look, gaze upon the glorious goodness that is God, meditate upon it, and be transformed into new people with a renewed vision for life.

Conclusion

THIS HAS INDEED BEEN a challenging journey through the minefields of contemporary ideology, a meta-critique of what is holding us back from the fullness of life in Christ. Take a deep breath. After unpacking some of the powerful and life-giving implications for culture formation and human flourishing in the incarnation, we are moving towards mature freedom and accountability. The logic of incarnation is clear and cogent. The good news is that God has not given up on us; he is calling us out of the crowd to try this amazing way of life, just as he did with Abraham and many others down the centuries. John the Baptist sensed the immensity of the situation when he prophetically announced Jesus's mission: "Look, the Lamb of God who takes away the sin of the world!" (John 1:29). Incarnation bridges relations on earth with relations in heaven; the Son of God has become the Son of Man. The Creator of the universe has taken on humanity. Our study of the incarnation reveals three interwoven ideas or doctrines: The Son of God as the Word of the Father; Incarnation of the Word; Restoration of a corrupted imago Dei by the Word. Incarnation and Redemption are interwoven. They are all about God drawing close and drawing us close through the most phenomenal offer of friendship. The writing of this book has refreshed and revitalized my personal faith, reminding me of how much God has shaped me through rigorous study of Scripture, many loving, wise mentors, including some of the greatest minds in the world. It also helped me see loving, worshiping believers in fresh relief. This constitutes a great crowd of witnesses. I am also thankful for many profound experiences of encounter with divine transcendence at various crossroads in my life.

It is so freeing and encouraging to realize the inclusivity of this incarnational spiritual culture. God's pursuit of wanderers and prodigals continues today. Many people indeed feel like they are in exile from God's goodness and glory, settling for a desert of no meaning beyond philosophical materialism and animal survival, individual choice and self-creation. They really feel that they are on their own—destined to carve out their own identity and destiny, alone. But God's glory and generosity has been revealed in the face of Jesus Christ as the most public, accessible truth. Incarnation argues strongly that we are not alone, that we have a spiritual home. The signs of transcendence are everywhere, but we must open our eyes and our hearts to perceive them with full consciousness. We have this tremendous opportunity to come out of the wilderness of our late modern age into the light, into God-kissed community and communion. It entails a deep soul-building adventure, living by the love, wisdom, and the power of the Holy Spirit—a new world with endless, fruitful promise. It turns out that God is our ultimate validator, savior and judge. His grace provides the continuity in our fragile selves; this brings us to a new level of articulacy to write the meaning of our story.

In the process of this exploration, we have talked much about presence, embodiment, transcendence, wisdom, narrative, servanthood, access to sources of the good and *agape* love. This high road adventure has been worth every effort to understand the grandeur and genius of God, to grapple with what the divine wants from us and for us. Thank you for joining me in this pilgrimage. I trust that you will agree that if we get the right perspective on life, we can renew our passion, live out of a robust identity and accomplish amazing things. There is no need to trash our faith in our cynical age. Once we experience transformation (enlargement) of our social imaginary, we can move forward boldly and with confidence. Our cynicism and skepticism will melt away, our nihilism will give way to rich purpose and meaning.

I have been deeply inspired by the *power of language to leverage the world*, the power of scholars, poets, and saints to show the constructive way forward, to bring us back on track to what is central, significant, and life-giving. The ancient Greek word *agape* is this kind of classic biblical term, a critical term with life-enhancing impact. It has a long and noble history, a spiritually wealthy heritage to deal with a host of human problems, anxieties, and existential identity problems. Athenian philosophers never heard about *agape*. During the Enlightenment, philosophers thought we could get along without *agape*, to live on universal reason alone. It is now clear that we cannot. Transcendent *agape* love transforms the self and then the world. This is the miracle of the Christian faith—that we can begin to exhibit the qualities and character of Christ. Love begins as otherworldly, grounded in

God as Trinity, far above human community (something radically other). Through the incarnation and the ongoing work of the Holy Spirit, it becomes deeply present and transformative within church, society, and culture. Jesus of Nazareth is the divine *Logos* that reveals to us the very mystery of our humanity, the divine Word who took on human flesh to offer us a new destiny and calling. The leap from non-living to living creaturehood is large, but the leap forward from animal awareness to *imago Dei* is truly immense.

We have discovered in our journey together the amazing possibility of a *transcendent turn* in philosophy that can set new cultural precedents. We have broken out of the confines of our time-space-energy-matter immanent frame to discover epiphany, an encounter with the largesse of the personal God himself, the ultimate source of all wisdom, love, and life. In the West, we have for too long nurtured a corrupt version of personal freedom—an *Enlightenment* devoid of responsibility, accountability, discernment of right and wrong, the virtuous life, good and evil, enduring covenants and commitments. This proves seriously inadequate to the cultural needs of the moment. *Agape* is a value-shaping principle, a whole new set of power relations, a creative work of divine presence and power (1 Cor 13). It provides a whole new footing for identity, a transfiguration of self, and transvaluation of values. It can and does unite our divided, fragmented world where it is cultivated, and allowed to flourish. But we must believe in God's superabundant love and grace for it to change us, to give us energy, resolve, and vision. Our personal stance, our *take*, remains enormously consequential.

David Bentley Hart noted that historically Christians have been known for their concern for the poor, the weak, and the infirmed and wishes to correct some popular, but misinformed, history. In this stance, he agrees with historian Tom Holland,[1] an atheist historian. Over the centuries, Christians have made huge, significant contributions to the culture of the contemporary hospital, including the famous Knights of St. John in the twelfth century. We have argued that this benevolent, incarnational humanism emerged because it was inspired and empowered by *agape* love. It was articulated and interpreted through the presence and sacrifices of Christ, and the work of the Holy Spirit. They realized a transcendent turn in their identity.

> There was . . . a long tradition of Christian monastic hospitals for
> the destitute and the dying, going back to the time of Constantine

1. Holland, *Dominion*.

and stretching from the Syrian and Byzantine East to the Western fringes of Christendom, a tradition that had no real precedent in pagan society. St Ephraim the Syrian (A.D 306–373), when the city of Edessa was ravaged by plague, established hospitals open to those who were afflicted. St. Basil the Great (A.D. 329–379) founded a hospital in Cappadocia with a ward set aside for the care of lepers, whom he did not disdain to nurse with his own hands. St. Benedict of Nursia (A.D. 480–547) opened a free infirmary at Monte Cassino and made care of the sick a paramount duty of the monks. . . . During the Middle Ages, the Benedictines alone were responsible for more than two thousand hospitals in Western Europe.[2]

Indeed, there seems to be much power in *agape* to change hearts, move planeloads of food and aid, protect children from abuse, provide education, fight for justice for victims and refugees worldwide. This can make a dramatic difference, it can move the world in noble ways that we all admire. Tom Holland warns cynical leaders that modern democracy, human rights, and universal benevolence owes much to Christianity for its inspiration and its philosophical floor. We should not treat the heritage lightly or cynically. Incarnational spiritual culture is resilient, but of course we have to diligently continue its cultivation.

Spiritual friendship is a priceless outworking of the incarnational spiritual culture. These mentors are people we can trust with our deepest secrets, people who have our back in time of trouble, people with whom we can both celebrate birth and mourn losses. New York City pastor Tim Keller noted in a sermon that, "All creation is about making us friends. It is a *divine conspiracy*. Christian redemption is about re-making or repairing our friendships, offering apologies, healing and forgiveness, making peace." That's a beautiful summary picture of God's intent of grace, gift, and goodness. Incarnational spiritual culture gives us real hope for a better self, a better family life, better leadership, a more positive platform for our lifelong vocational contribution. It codes tremendous hope for the future within our story, beyond anything artificial intelligence can hope to offer.[3]

God is in the process of changing people's stories from poorer to richer, from harsher to gentler, rigid to flexible, sadder to joyful, shameful to confident. Spiritual friendship and spiritual direction is a key player in this transformation. He is patiently waiting for us to respond to his call of

2. Hart, *Atheist Delusions*, 30.
3. Lennox, *2084*, 196.

grace, for us to partner with him in the task of becoming *shalom*, a conduit of blessing to the whole earth and its peoples. In God's economy, no one is unimportant, everyone's personhood and giftedness matters in the kingdom enterprise. Curt Thompson captures the move from disengagement to attachment, mindlessness to mindfulness:

> God creates systems that reflect his heart desire that the world be populated with individuals exuding joy, peace, patience, kindness, goodness and faithfulness, gentleness and self-control. When practiced in community, those virtues inexorably emerge as justice and mercy, two biblical pillars of politics and economics.[4]

Love is our calling through *I-Thou* encounter. It is a dialogue initiated by God: *Where are you speaking from?* It cannot be reduced to an obligation, but ultimately grows into our joy. It is the very bedrock of everything, and this superabundant love is grounded in Christ who has taken on human flesh to save us from ourselves, to restore the corrupted human *imago Dei*. It is a paradigm shift to discover that the whole universe and everything in it is grounded in love, in a holy God who is fullness of compassion and grace, truth and justice. When we seriously explore an incarnational spiritual culture, it offers us an abundance of public evidence for a new outlook, for stirring our imagination towards a new narrative journey. God wants to transform us into a new transcultural spiritual culture, where we have multicultural flexibility to follow his way of holiness as our life journey towards Christlikeness. The ethos is bold but humble, confident but generous, filled with gratitude and joy. Incarnational spiritual culture is what God is saving us into, transforming us into. God be praised, Father, Son, and Holy Spirit, for the unspeakable, miraculous gift of the incarnation.

4. Thompson, *Anatomy of the Soul*, 238.

Addendum

What Do People Mean
by a Personal Relationship with Jesus?

THIS IS TRULY A profound question and one of the dramatic implications of the incarnation. Another key question is raised by the Danish philosopher Søren Kierkegaard, "What do I find in my deepest core to be true?" On reflection, he saw the answer as self-sacrificial love (*agape*) found in Jesus of Nazareth. For Kierkegaard, God was his way out of anxiety and despair. Here was the *truth that edifies*. Philosopher Immanuel Kant saw, especially in his third tome on practical reason, that the *existential human need* was for justice and the good to prevail, and only a being such as an omni-benevolent and powerful God was adequate to secure that guarantee. There had to be a cosmic will for human goodness to prevail. We have argued in this book that this works well within the culture of incarnational spirituality. This source of the good in God would lead us to always treat others as an end in themselves, rather than a selfish means to our benefit. I remember a philosopher who once noted, "God from ancient times (Plato and Aristotle) is the central explanatory concept. If you don't understand this concept, you don't understand the first thing about the world. Even the notorious atheist Nietzsche recognized this truth."

> *Agape* is a prophetic love. It refuses to equate anyone with his immediate observable being. A human being is not deeply and essentially the same as the one who is visible to the employer, neighbor, salesman, policeman, judge, friend or spouse. A human being is destined to live in eternity and is fully known only to God.

> *Agape* is about the spiritual destiny of the individual; destiny is
> a spiritual drama. My destiny is my own selfhood given by God,
> but given not as an established reality, like a rock or a hill, but as
> a task lying under divine imperative. . . . Agape is simply the af-
> firmation of this paradox and of this destiny underlying it. Agape
> looks beyond all marks of fallenness, all traits by which people are
> judged and ranked, and acknowledges the glory each person—as
> envisioned in Christian faith—gains from the creative mercy of
> God. It sets aside the most astute worldly judgment in behalf of
> destiny.[1]

The individual self (soul/person), as we have seen, is elevated by this love, affirmed in its destiny. *Agape* informs the good and the qualities of the will. It makes up for human weakness and selfishness. Trinitarian goodness empowers, clarifies, and animates the human self in its quest for true and sound spiritual identity and wholeness. It acknowledges the value that each person gains from recognition, mercy, healing, and affirmation by God. Within this frame, the individual person engages this transforming love from the divine Other.

When I was dating my wife, I wanted to spend as much time as pos-sible with her. Why was this the case? Because I wanted to get to know her better. I wanted to know what she liked, her values, and her character. I wanted to get to know her sense of humor, her pet peeves, her passion. It turned out that our stories overlapped in significant ways. Her vision for life, her sense of calling was also of vital interest. I soon realized that they would creatively align with mine. That seemed like a small miracle at the time. We had fun exploring each other's nuances and personality, hearing each other's stories and laughing about the adventures in mountain climb-ing, travel, and work with students. Our curiosity admittedly was a little intense: I wanted to know everything. Was she the one? During this time, I had to learn how to make choices that showed her that I loved her, that is, if the relationship was going to be a serious one with depth and sincerity.

The journey was not all roses, but it was very creative and fun. This transition in life also involved some sacrifice of my interests, time and goals as a single man. I mused: How could I possibly integrate this complex, in-triguing person into my already busy life? For example, to prove my interest in her joy of adventure and trekking, I did a six-day hike with a group she helped guide in the Grand Canyon. Our love and mutual curiosity pushed

---

1. Tinder, *Political Meaning of Christianity*, 25, 28.

me out of my comfort zone and into new experience of magnificent wonder and challenge. Clearly, I was going to have to grow and change, move to the next level of outdoor activity. That was a tough hike with temperatures reaching 116 degrees Fahrenheit at the bottom of the canyon, complete with rattlesnakes and scorpions. Every day, I was reminded of the biblical Exodus story—water was a premium for our survival. Would I make it out? In retrospect, six days was much better than forty years.

But this is what happens when you love someone: You want a close, intimate, and personal relationship with openness, harmony, and honesty between you. When it happens, it is magical. You really want to learn about and explore life together and bring your individual histories together. You learn how to work together and participate in each other's giftedness. You also push each other to risk new experiences, think new thoughts, growing into a new outlook as a couple. I also quickly realized that this precious relationship had to be protected. An intimate friendship is also very special, because you can share your burdens and joys, weaknesses and strengths, without fear of rejection or judgment. You can laugh and cry together, spend time in comradery, go through tough experiences together. You help each other to grow, to stay in the game of life when it gets tough and complex. A conversation partnership within which you can trust the deeper things of your heart, including doubts and uncertainties, is worth its weight in gold. One might even suggest that this is essential to one's existential wellbeing. God knew what he was doing in his concern to incarnate his love; he has shown that we were not created to be alone, but rather to thrive in community. We become more fully human in a network of persons, a communion of friends aspiring to the good, the excellent, and praiseworthy.

In many respects, the same goes for a relationship with Jesus. If you are looking into it out of curiosity, this means you aspire to learn about and follow him and learn from his teaching. You want to take him seriously in all that he represents and reveals about reality and about God's character. It is no small adventure. You are open to the vulnerability of discovering the things he might reveal about your character as well—even your dark secrets. The Bible clearly indicates that you are generously invited to have a close, intimate, and personal relationship with him. You are invited to take on his mission to make a better world, to live to a higher standard. It truly is an amazing opportunity to get to know the God who created you, and to find personal freedom in a covenant relationship with Messiah Jesus. But what does this mean and how does it actually work?

When you investigate Jesus and his claims and then choose him as your mentor, you start on a lifelong adventure of faith, an enticing journey with many surprises. This opens up life in unique and creative ways. You can also take yourself more seriously and discover more of what you have to offer the world. You discover the incredible fact that you are loved by God himself. This relationship is lived out in prayer, worship, and fellowship, Bible study and mercy ministry with others. You find yourself wanting to practice the virtues which are rooted in love, gratitude, and humility. You start caring more about the interests of others. You may find yourself practicing justice, caring for the poor, the prisoner, the needy. In many ways, it will reshape your whole world and set of values and goals (*transvaluation of your values*).

Following Jesus sets higher ideals of life lived for others, addressing human suffering and other existential concerns like meaning, identity, and purpose. As you claim Jesus as your personal Lord and guide, and accept God's wisdom as your foundation, you will discover new horizons. It will engage your history and experience, help you to make sense of your past, address your pain, and heal your brokenness. You will soon feel the security of his love, wisdom, and direction, with less time spent chasing false dreams and asking for forgiveness. As with any healthy relationship, it starts with receptivity. You choose how vulnerable you want to be. It's a choice only you can make, but one that makes a real existential difference. Following the Jesus Way involves a new stance towards the world. Your parents or grandparents cannot choose faith for you. Nor can a friend choose for you. They can begin the introduction and inspire you about the promise, the hope and meaning they now experience. But the first leap of faith is all up to you.

At this juncture, I want to mention a caution. Some people choose a mere intellectual view of God, but this is not yet a *personal* relationship. An intimate relationship must be cultivated in faith and humility, with a longer-term commitment that engages your whole life. It sets out new priorities. Some like the idea of an all-powerful, benevolent Being, but still want to be autonomous in living for their own interests. They think about what belief in God can do for them. To intellectually know *about* Jesus, or have an admiration *for* Jesus is fine and good. But this does not constitute the full reality of discipleship, which is what we all hope for in a lasting divine friendship. There is much more color and texture to a robust relationship that involves obedience to his teaching on life and personal stewardship.

Love comes with expectations. Once we start investigating his story, many of us have lots of questions. That's normal because there is much to process in his identity, teaching, and claims, plus the implications of a covenant relationship with God. Some things are shocking, but good. Darrell Johnson articulates this so well in *Who Is Jesus?*[2] C. S. Lewis may also help you make sense of things. Tim Keller has clarified many hard questions in *Reason for God* and *Making Sense of God*.[3] You may also have heard about the *Alpha Course*, which is an introductory round-table discussion on faith and its nuances in a safe environment, where all inquiring questions are welcome and respected.

Giftedness, as depicted in Rom 12 and Eph 4, will be released in you to accomplish things you may never have thought possible. A *new you* emerges. Jesus will guide you into freedom from previous obsessions and addictions. With him, you can exchange your stress and anxiety for *shalom*. Through forgiveness and reconciliation, he will lead you into relational and communal health and spiritual wholeness. Most of all, Jesus leads us to become people of character who are able to face the challenges of life with courage, realism, and optimism, people who are able to grapple with problems constructively. Former University of British Columbia president, Dr. Santa Ono, believes that faith in Jesus can add so much to our mental health and general wellbeing. It certainly made a dramatic difference in his life, moving him from despair to hope as a student. Jesus showed this concern for us most dramatically when he died on the cross. Who could imagine that any human being could express such love?

John 1:1–18 shows how Jesus, although God, made himself accessible to us. The *Word became flesh* and journeyed with us, lived with us, shared our humanity in the most profound event of human history. The Creator joined his creatures on planet earth in an amazing self-humbling, self-sacrificial exercise (Phil 2). But we must *choose* Jesus in good faith, receive the gift of his revelation, his sacrifice. We can expose ourselves to his moral light, engage in the kind of lifestyle he offers, empowered by superabundant grace. Faith is a grateful response to such a gift. Being able to say *yes* to Jesus is only possible because God has chosen, called, and pursued us first. He has had his eye on you for a long time. He has good intentions towards you. He invites you into his family (Eph 1). Abraham Joshua Heschel in his writing has shown that God is deeply invested in human beings and that

2. Johnson, *Who Is Jesus?*
3. Keller, *Reason for God*; Keller, *Making Sense of God.*

he will never give up on them. That often comes as a stunning realization for many people: that God invites us into conversation and ultimately into friendship and divine communion. That's a lot to get your head around and it will take time. I am assured that Jesus is the *Yes* and *Amen* to it all, the best empirical evidence we have of a loving God who cares about the whole world, including you, your friends, and family. I highly recommend this journey from my own personal experience.

Bibliography

Adams, Robert Merrihew. *Finite and Infinite Goods: A Framework for Ethics*. Oxford: Oxford University Press, 1999.

Alexander, Denis, and Alister McGrath, eds. *Coming to Faith through Dawkins: 12 Essays on the Pathway from New Atheism to Christianity*. Grand Rapids, MI: Kregel, 2023.

Balthasar, Hans Urs. *Theo-Drama: Theological Dramatic Theory*. San Francisco: Ignatius, 1993.

Barton, Ruth Haley. *Sacred Rhythms: Arranging Our Lives for Spiritual Transformation*. Downers Grove, IL: InterVarsity, 2006.

———. *Strengthening the Soul of Your Leadership: Seeing God in the Crucible of Ministry*. Downers Grove, IL: InterVarsity, 2008.

Becker, Ernest. *The Denial of Death*. New York: Free Press, 1997.

Bouma-Prediger, Steven. *For the Beauty of the Earth: A Christian Vision of Creation Care (Engaging Culture)*. Grand Rapids, MI: Baker Academic, 2001.

Braun, Gabriele G. *God's Praise and God's Presence: A Biblical-Theological Study*. Eugene, OR: Wipf & Stock, 2020.

Brooks, David. *The Road to Character*. New York: Random House, 2015.

———. *The Second Mountain: The Quest for a Moral Life*. New York: Random House, 2020.

Brown, Brené. *Rising Strong*. New York: Spiegel & Grau, 2015.

Brown, W. S., and Brad Strawn. *The Physical Nature of Christianity: Neuroscience, Psychology, and the Church*. Cambridge: Cambridge University Press, 2012.

Brueggemann, Walter. *A Gospel of Hope*. Louisville, KT: Westminster John Knox, 2018.

Buber, Martin. *I and Thou*. New York: Scribner's, 2010.

Buechner, Frederick. *The Longing for Home: Recollections and Reflections*. New York: HarperCollins, 1996.

Calhoun, A. A. *Invitations from God: Accepting God's Offer to Rest, Weep, Forgive, Wait, Remember and More*. Downers Grove, IL: InterVarsity, 2011.

Carkner, Gordon E. "A Critical Examination of Michel Foucault's Concept of Moral Self-Constitution in Dialogue with Charles Taylor." PhD diss., University of Wales, 2006.

———. "Charles Taylor and the Myth of the Secular." *YouTube*, February 11, 2022. https://www.youtube.com/watch?v=f4KZhWc2TDY.

———. *The Great Escape from Nihilism: Rediscovering our Passion in Late Modernity*. Abbotsford, BC: InFocus, 2016.

———. *Mapping the Future: Arenas of Discipleship and Spiritual Formation*. Abbotsford, BC: InFocus, 2018.

———. "Science & Scientism: Oxford Biophysicist Ard Louis." *YouTube*, April 7, 2022. https://www.youtube.com/watch?v=1IzPcRQ3r9A.

———. "What Is Truth and Why Does It Matter?" https://ubcgcu.org/2021/05/27/what-is-truth-and-why-does-it-matter/.

Carlin, John. *Playing the Enemy: Nelson Mandela and the Game that Made a Nation*. New York: Penguin, 2008.

Cavanaugh, William T. *Being Consumed: Economics and Christian Desire*. Grand Rapids, MI: Eerdmans, 2008.

———. *The Uses of Idolatry*. Oxford: Oxford University Press, 2024.

Connolly, William E. "Michel Foucault: An Exchange: Taylor, Foucault, and Otherness." *Political Theory* 13 (1985) 365–76.

Crawford, Matthew B. *The World Beyond Your Head: On Becoming an Individual in an Age of Distraction*. New York: Farrar, Strauss & Giroux, 2015.

Crouch, Andy. *Culture Making: Recovering Our Creative Calling*. Downers Grove, IL: InterVarsity, 2008.

Davison, Andrew P. *Astrobiology and Christian Doctrine: Exploring the Implications of Life in the Universe*. Cambridge: Cambridge University Press, 2023.

Delsol, Chantal. *Icarus Fallen: The Search for Meaning in an Uncertain World*. Translated by Robin Dick. Wilmington, DE: ISIS, 2003.

Eagleton, Terry. *The Ideology of the Aesthetic*. Hoboken, NJ: Wiley-Blackwell, 1991.

Ehrenberg, Alain. *The Weariness of the Self: Diagnosing the History of Depression in the Contemporary Age*. Montreal: McGill-Queen's University Press, 2010.

Faulk, Frank. "C. S. Lewis and the Inklings, Part 1." *CBC Radio*, October 9, 2013. https://www.cbc.ca/radio/ideas/c-s-lewis-and-the-inklings-part-1-1.2914250.

Favale, Abigail. *The Genesis of Gender: A Christian Theory*. San Francisco: Ignatius, 2022.

Foster, Richard. *Celebration of Discipline: The Path to Spiritual Growth*. San Francisco: HarperSanFrancisco, 1998.

Gawronski, Raymond. *Word and Silence: Hans Urs Von Balthasar and the Spiritual Encounter between East and West*. New York: T. & T. Clark, 1995.

Girard, René. "Dionysus versus the Crucified." *MLN* 99 (1984) 816–35.

———. *I See Satan Fall Like Lightning*. Ossining, NY: Orbis, 2001.

Gould, Paul. *Cultural Apologetics: Renewing the Christian Voice, Conscience and Imagination in a Disenchanted World*. Grand Rapids, MI: Zondervan, 2019.

Granberg-Michaelson, Wesley. *A Worldly Spirituality: the Call to Care for the Earth*. San Francisco: Harper & Row, 1984.

Green, Michael, and Gordon Carkner. *Ten Myths about Christianity*. Oxford: Lion, 1988.

Greenleaf, Robert K. *The Power of Servant Leadership*. San Francisco: Berrett-Koehler, 1998.

Hansen, Colin. *Timothy Keller: His Spiritual and Intellectual Formation*. Grand Rapids, MI: Zondervan, 2022.

Harari, Yuval Noah. *21 Lessons for the 21st Century*. New York: Signal, 2018.

Harris, Sam. *The Moral Landscape: How Science Can Determine Human Values*. New York: Free Press, 2011.

Hart, David Bentley. *Atheist Delusions: the Christian Revolution and Its Fashionable Enemies*. New Haven, CT: Yale University Press, 2009.

———. *The Experience of God: Being, Consciousness, Bliss*. New Haven, CT: Yale University Press, 2013.

Heschel, Abraham Joshua. *The Wisdom of Heschel*. New York: Farrar, Straus & Giroux, 1975.

Holland, Tom. *Dominion: How the Christian Revolution Remade the World*. New York: Basic, 2019.

Houston, James M., and Jens Zimmermann, eds. *Sources of the Christian Self: A Cultural History of Christian Identity*. Grand Rapids, MI: Eerdmans, 2018.

Hunter, James Davison. *To Change the World: the Irony, Tragedy and Possibility of Christianity in the Late Modern World*. Oxford: Oxford University Press, 2010.

Hunter, James Davison, and Paul Nedelisky. *Science and the Good: The Tragic Quest for Moral Foundations*. New Haven, CT: Yale University Press, 2018.

Johnson, Darrell W. *Who Is Jesus?* Vancouver, BC: Regent College Publishing, 2011.

Kaiser, Walter C., Jr. *The Promise Plan of God: A Biblical Theology of Old and New Testaments*. Grand Rapids, MI: Zondervan Academic, 2008.

Keller, Tim. *Making Sense of God: An Invitation to the Skeptical*. New York: Viking, 2016.

———. *The Reason for God: Belief in an Age of Skepticism*. New York: Penguin, 2009.

Kreeft, Peter. *Making Sense Out of Suffering*. Servant, 1986.

Lennox, John. *2084: Artificial Intelligence and the Future of Humanity*. Grand Rapids, MI: Zondervan, 2020.

Lewis, C. S. *Mere Christianity*. Glasgow, Scot.: Collins, 1984.

Loconte, Joseph. *A Hobbit, a Wardrobe, and a Great War: How J. R. R. Tolkien and C. S. Lewis Rediscovered Faith, Friendship, and Heroism in the Cataclysm of 1914–18*. Nashville, TN: Nelson, 2015.

Long, D. Stephen. *The Goodness of God: Theology, the Church and Social Order*. Grand Rapids, MI: Brazos, 2001.

———. *Speaking of God: Theology, Language and Truth*. Grand Rapids: Eerdmans, 2009.

Malik, Charles. *A Christian Critique of the University*. Waterloo, ON: North Waterloo Academic, 1987.

McFadyen, Alistair I. "Sins of Praise: The Assault on God's Freedom." In *God & Freedom: Essays in Historical and Systematic Theology*, edited by Colin Gunton, 36–56. Edinburgh, UK: T. & T. Clark, 1995.

McLeish, Tom. *Faith and Wisdom in Science*. Oxford: Oxford University Press, 2016.

———. *The Poetry and Music of Science: Comparing Creativity in Science and Art*. Oxford: Oxford University Press, 2019.

McMinn, Mark R. *The Science of Virtue: Why Positive Psychology Matters to the Church*. Grand Rapids, MI: Brazos, 2017.

Merton, Thomas. *New Seeds of Contemplation*. New York: New Directions, 1986.

Middleton, J. Richard. *The Liberating Image: The Imago Dei in Genesis 1*. Grand Rapids, MI: Brazos, 2005.

———. "A New Earth Perspective." In *Four Views on Heaven*, edited by Michael E. Witter et al., 65–94. Counterpoints: Bible and Theology. Grand Rapids: Zondervan Academic, 2022.

Milbank, John. *Theology and Social Theory: Beyond Secular Reason*. Oxford: Blackwell, 1993.

Moltmann, Jurgen. *The Spirit of Life. A Universal Affirmation*. London: SCM, 1992.

———. *Theology of Hope*. London: SCM, 1993.

Mongrain, Kevin. *The Systematic Thought of Hans Urs von Balthasar: An Irenaen Retrieval*. New York: Crossroad, 2002.

Myers, Jimmy. "Is It True that 'The World Will Be Saved by Beauty'?" *First Things*, July 25, 2015. https://www.firstthings.com/web-exclusives/2015/07/student-essay-contest-winner-first-place.

Newbigin, Lesslie. *Truth to Tell: the Gospel as Public Truth*. Grand Rapids, MI: Eerdmans, 1991.

O'Donovan, Oliver. *Resurrection and Moral Order: An Outline for Evangelical Ethics*. 2nd ed. Grand Rapids: Eerdmans, 1994.

Page, Don. *Servant-Empowered Leadership*. Langley, BC: Power to Change, 2009.

Palmer, Parker J. *Let Your Life Speak: Listening to the Voice of Vocation*. Hoboken, NJ: Wiley, 1999.

Peck, M. Scott. *The Road Less Travelled: A New Psychology of Love, Traditional Values and Spiritual Growth*. New York: Simon & Schuster, 1978.

Peterson, Eugene. *The Jesus Way: A Conversation in the Ways that Jesus Is the Way*. Grand Rapids, MI: Eerdmans, 2007.

———. *Practice Resurrection: A Conversation on Growing Up in Christ*. Grand Rapids, MI: Eerdmans, 2010.

Plantinga, Alvin. *Where the Conflict Really Lies: Science, Religion and Naturalism*. Oxford: Oxford University Press, 2011.

Postema, Don. *Space for God: Study and Practice of Spirituality and Prayer*. Grand Rapids, MI: CRC, 1992.

Ricoeur, Paul. *Oneself as Another*. Chicago: University of Chicago Press, 1992.

Sacks, Jonathan. *The Dignity of Difference: How to Avoid the Clash of Civilizations*. London: Continuum, 2002.

———. *Not in God's Name: Confronting Religious Violence*. New York: Schocken, 2015.

Sayers, Mark. *Disappearing Church: From Cultural Relevance to Gospel Resilience*. Chicago: Moody, 2016.

Schneewind, Jerome B. *The Invention of Autonomy: A History of Modern Moral Philosophy*. Cambridge: Cambridge University Press, 1998.

Schrag, Calvin O. *The Self after Postmodernity*. New Haven, CT: Yale University Press, 1997.

Schwöbel, Christoph. "God's Goodness and Human Morality." In *God: Action and Revelation*, by Christoph Schwöbel, 63–82. Kampen, Holl.: Pharos, 1992.

———. "Imago Libertatis: Human and Divine Freedom." In *God & Freedom: Essays in Historical and Systematic Theology*, edited by Colin Gunton, 57–81. Edinburgh: T. & T. Clark, 1995.

Scruton, Roger. *On Human Nature*. Princeton, NJ: Princeton University Press, 2017.

Shepherd, Andrew. *The Gift of the Other: Lévinas, Derrida and a Theology of Hospitality*. Eugene, OR: Pickwick, 2014.

Siedentop, Larry. *Inventing the Individual: The Origins of Western Liberalism*. Cambridge, MA: Belknap, 2015.

Smith, Christian. *Atheist Overreach: Why Atheism Cannot Deliver*. Oxford: Oxford University Press, 2018.

Smith, James K. A. *The Nicene Option: An Incarnational Phenomenology*. Waco, TX: Baylor University Press, 2021.

———. *On the Road with Saint Augustine: A Real-World Spirituality for Restless Hearts*. Grand Rapids, MI: Brazos, 2019.

———. *You Are What You Love: The Spiritual Power of Habit*. Grand Rapids, MI: Brazos, 2016.

Soltes, Eugene. *Why They Do It: Inside the Mind of the White Collar Criminal.* New York: Public Affairs, 2016.

Taylor, Charles. *A Catholic Modernity? Charles Taylor's Marianist Award Lecture.* With responses by William M. Shea, Rosemary Luling Haughton, George Marsden, and Jean Bethke Elshtain. Edited by James L. Heft. Oxford: Oxford University Press, 1999.

———. *The Language Animal: The Full Shape of the Human Linguistic Capacity.* Cambridge, MS: Harvard University Press, 2016.

———. *A Secular Age.* Cambridge, MA: Harvard University Press, 2007.

———. *Sources of the Self: The Making of the Modern Identity.* Cambridge, MA: Harvard University Press, 1989.

Thiselton, Anthony C. *Interpreting God and the Postmodern Self: on Meaning, Manipulation and Promise.* Edinburgh: T. & T. Clark, 1995.

Thompson, Curt. *Anatomy of the Soul: Surprising Connections between Neuroscience and Spiritual Practices that Can Transform Your Life and Relationships.* Carol Stream, IL: Tyndale, 2010.

Tinder, Glenn. *The Political Meaning of Christianity: An Interpretation.* Eugene, OR: Wipf & Stock, 2000.

Treier, Daniel T. "Incarnation." In *Christian Dogmatics: Reformed Theology for the Church Catholic,* edited by Michael Allen and Scott R. Swain, 216–42. Grand Rapids, MI: Baker Academic, 2016.

Trueman, Carl R. *The Rise and Triumph of the Modern Self: Cultural Amnesia, Expressive Individualism and the Road to the Sexual Revolution.* Wheaton, IL: Crossway, 2020.

Vanhoozer, Kevin J. *Is There a Meaning in This Text? The Bible, the Reader, and the Morality of Literary Knowledge.* Grand Rapids, MI: Zondervan, 2009.

Voegelin, Eric. *The New Science of Politics: An Introduction.* Chicago: University of Chicago Press, 1987.

———. *Science, Politics and Gnosticism: Two Essays.* Washington, DC: Regnery, 1968.

Volf, Miroslav. *After Our Likeness: The Church as the Image of the Trinity.* Grand Rapids, MI: Eerdmans, 1998.

———. *Exclusion and Embrace: A Theological Exploration of Identity, Otherness and Reconciliation.* Nashville, TN: Abingdon, 1996.

———. *Flourishing: Why We Need Religion in a Globalizing World.* New Haven, CT: Yale University Press, 2015.

Wallis, Jim. *The (Un)Common Good: How the Gospel Brings Hope to a World Divided.* Grand Rapids, MI: Brazos, 2014.

Ward, Michael. *Planet Narnia: The Seven Heavens in the Imagination of C. S. Lewis.* Oxford: Oxford University Press, 2007.

Watkin, Christopher. *Biblical Critical Theory: How the Bible's Unfolding Story Makes Sense of Modern Life and Culture.* Grand Rapids, MI: Zondervan Academic, 2022.

Weber, Carolyn. *Surprised by Oxford: A Memoir.* Nashville, TN: Nelson, 2011.

White, Randy. *Encountering God in the City: Onramps to Personal and Community Transformation.* Downers Grove, IL: InterVarsity, 2006.

Willard, Dallas. *The Divine Conspiracy: Rediscovering Our Hidden Life in God.* HarperSanFrancisco, 1998.

———. *Renovation of the Heart: Putting on the Character of Christ.* Carol Stream, IL: Tyndale, 2002.

Williams, Daniel K. *The Politics of the Cross: A Christian Alternative to Partisanship.* Grand Rapids, MI: Eerdmans, 2021.

Williams, Rowan. *The Truce of God: Peacemaking in Troubled Times*. Grand Rapids, MI: Eerdmans, 2005.

Wolterstorff, Nicholas. *In This World of Wonders: Memoir of a Life in Learning*. Grand Rapids, MI: Eerdmans, 2019.

Wright, N. T. *The Challenge of Jesus: Discovering Who Jesus Was and Is*. Downers Grove, IL: InterVarsity, 2015.

———. *Simply Christian: Why Christianity Makes Sense*. New York: HarperCollins, 2010.

———. *Surprised by Hope: Rethinking Heaven, the Resurrection, and the Mission of the Church*. New York: HarperOne, 2008.

Yancey, Philip. *The Jesus I Never Knew*. Grand Rapids, MI: Zondervan, 2002.

Zagzebski, Linda. *Virtues of the Mind: An Inquiry into the Nature of Virtue and the Ethical Foundations of Knowledge*. Cambridge: Cambridge University Press, 1996.

Zimmermann, Jens. *Dietrich Bonhoeffer's Christian Humanism*. Oxford: Oxford University Press, 2019.

———. *Hermeneutics: A Very Short Introduction*. Oxford: Oxford University Press, 2015.

———. *Humanism and Religion: A Call to Renewal of Western Culture*. Oxford: Oxford University Press, 2012.

———. *Incarnational Humanism: A Philosophy of Culture for the Church in the World*. Downers Grove, IL: InterVarsity Academic, 2012.